BIOLOGY
FOR DOUBLE SCIENCE

David Applin

Hodder & Stoughton
A MEMBER OF THE HODDER HEADLINE GROUP

A catalogue record for this title is available from the British Library.

ISBN 0340 775645

First published 2000

Impression number 10 9 8 7 6 5 4 3 2 1
Year 2005 2004 2003 2002 2001 2000

Copyright © David Applin
Copyright © pp 4-6 Tony Buzan

Mind Map® is the registered trade mark of the Buzan Organisation.

All rights reserved. No part of this publication may be reproduced or transmitted in any form or by any means, electronic or mechanical, including photocopy, recording, or any information storage and retrieval system, without permission in writing from the publisher or under licence from the Copyright Licensing Agency Limited. Further details of such licences (for reprographic reproduction) may be obtained from the Copyright Licensing Agency Limited, 90 Tottenham Court Road, London W1P 9HE.

Editorial, design and production by Hart McLeod, Cambridge

Printed in Spain by Graphycems for Hodder & Stoughton Educational, a division of Hodder Headline Plc, 338 Euston Road, London NW1 3BH

Contents

Revision Rescue 4

Living things and the environment 7

Characteristics of life 7
Life on Earth 8
Classification 9
Identifying living things 10
Looking at an ecosystem 11
Food chains 13
Food webs 14
Ecological pyramids 15
Decomposition and cycles 18
Distribution of organisms 20
Population size 21
Producing food 22
Pollution 23
Living things and the environment quiz 25

Cells 26

Cell structure 26
Molecules on the move 27
Cells, tissues and organs 29
Cell division 30
Mitosis and meiosis – sequence of events 31
Comparing mitosis and meiosis 32
Chemicals in living things – carbohydrates 33
Lipids and proteins 34
Nucleic acids 35
Enzymes in action 36
Enzymes 37
Cells quiz 38

Plants as organisms 39

Photosynthesis 39
Inside the leaf 40
Transport in plants 41
Plant responses 46
Plants as organisms quiz 48

Humans as organisms: energy and transport 49

Food 49
Digesting food 51
Digestive enzymes 54
Using air 55
Breathing movements 58
Respiration 59
Blood 60
Moving blood around 61
Blood vessels 62
Capillaries 63
Disorders of the blood 64
Humans as organisms: energy and transport quiz 66

Humans as organisms: coordination, control and disease 67

Coordination and the nervous system 67
Reflex arc 68
Hormones 69
The menstrual cycle 70
Regulating glucose 71
Homeostasis 72
The skin and control of body temperature 75
What is disease? 78
Lifestyles and disease 79
Fighting disease 80
Humans as organisms: coordination, control and disease quiz 82

Inheritance and evolution 83

Reproduction 83
Monohybrid inheritance 86
Inheritance of sex 88
Sex-linked inheritance 89
Genetic engineering 90
Variation 92
Evolution 94
Inheritance and evolution quiz 96

Revision Rescue

The pages that follow contain a gold mine of information on how you can achieve success in your exams. Read them and apply the information, and you will be able to spend less, but more efficient, time studying, with better results.

This section gives you vital information on how to remember more while you are learning and how to remember more after you have finished studying. It explains

- how to use special techniques to improve your memory
- how to use a revolutionary note-taking technique called Mind Mapping that will double your memory and help you to write essays and answer exam questions
- how to read everything faster while at the same time improving your comprehension and concentration

Your amazing memory

There are five important things you must know about your brain and memory to revolutionise your school life.

1. how your memory ('recall') works while you are learning
2. how your memory works after you have finished learning
3. how to use Mind Maps – a special technique for helping you with all aspects of your studies
4. how to increase your reading speed
5. how to zap your revision

1 Recall during learning – the need for breaks

When you are studying, your memory can concentrate, understand and remember well for between 20 and 45 minutes at a time. Then it needs a break. If you carry on for longer than this without one, your memory starts to break down! If you study for hours non-stop, you will remember only a fraction of what you have been trying to learn, and you will have wasted valuable revision time.

So, ideally, study for less than an hour, then take a five- to ten-minute break. During the break listen to music, go for a walk, do some exercise, or just daydream. (Daydreaming is a necessary brain-power booster – geniuses do it regularly.) During the break your brain will be sorting out what it has been learning, and you will go back to your books with the new information safely stored and organised in your memory banks.

2 Recall after learning – the waves of your memory

What do you think begins to happen to your memory straight after you have finished learning something? Does it immediately start forgetting? No! Your brain actually increases its power and carries on remembering. For a short time after your study session, your brain integrates the information, making a more complete picture of everything it has just learnt. Only then does the rapid decline in memory begin, and as much as 80 per cent of what you have learnt can be forgotten in a day.

However, if you catch the top of the wave of your memory, and briefly review (look back over) what you have been revising at the correct time, the memory is stamped in far more strongly, and stays at the crest of the wave for a much longer time. To maximise your brain's power to remember, take a few minutes and use a Mind Map to review what you have learnt at the end of a day. Then review it at the end of a week, again at the end of the month, and finally a week before the exams. That way you'll ride your memory wave all the way to your exam – and beyond!

Amazing as your memory is (think of everything you actually have stored in your brain at this moment) the principles on which it operates are very simple. Your brain will remember if it:

(a) has an image (a picture or a symbol);

(b) has that image fixed

(c) can link that image to something else.

3 The Mind Map® – a picture of the way you think

Do you like taking notes? More importantly, do you like having to go back over and learn them before exams? Most students I know certainly do not! And how do you take your notes? Most people take notes on lined paper, using blue or black ink. The result, visually, is boring! And what does your brain do when it is bored? It turns off, tunes out, and goes to sleep! Add a dash of colour, rhythm, imagination, and the whole note-taking process becomes much more fun, uses more of your brain's abilities, and improves your recall and understanding.

A Mind Map mirrors the way your brain works. It can be used for note-taking from books or in class, for reviewing what you have just studied, for revising, and for essay planning for coursework and in exams. It uses all your memory's natural techniques to build up your rapidly growing 'memory muscle'.

You will find sample Mind Maps throughout this book. Study them, add some colour, personalise them, and then have a go at drawing your own – you'll remember them far better! Put them on your walls and in your files for a quick-and-easy review of the topic.

How to draw a Mind Map®

1 Start in the middle of the page with the page turned sideways. This gives your brain the maximum room for its thoughts.

2 Always start by drawing a small picture or symbol. Why? Because a picture is worth a thousand words to your brain. And try to use at least three colours, as colour helps your memory even more.

3 Let your thoughts flow, and write or draw your ideas on coloured branching lines connected to your central image. These key symbols and words are the headings for your topic.

4 Then add facts and ideas by drawing more, smaller, branches on to the appropriate main branches, just like a tree.

5 Always print your word clearly on its line. Use only one word per line.

6 To link ideas and on different branches, use arrows, colours, underlining and boxes.

How to read a Mind Map®

1 Begin in the centre, the focus of your topic.

2 The words/images attached to the centre are like chapter headings, so read them next.

3 Always read out from the centre, in every direction (even on the left-hand side, where you will have to read from right to left, instead of the usual left to right).

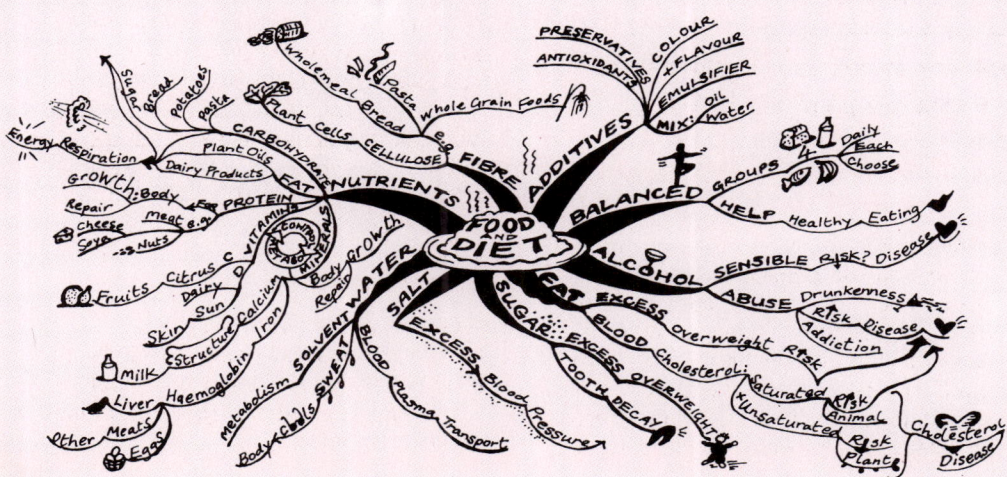

4 Super speed reading

It seems incredible, but it's been proved – the faster you read, the more you understand and remember! So here are some tips to help you to practise reading faster – you'll cover the ground more quickly, remember more, and have more time for revision!

First read the whole text (whether it's a lengthy book or an exam paper) very quickly, to give your brain an overall idea of what's ahead and get it working. (It's like sending out a scout to look at the territory you have to cover – it's much easier when you know what to expect!) Then read the text again for more detailed information.

Have the text a reasonable distance away from your eyes. In this way your eye/brain system will be able to see more at a glance, and will naturally begin to read faster.

Take in groups of words at a time. Rather than reading 'slowly and carefully' read faster, more enthusiastically. Your comprehension will rocket!

Take in phrases rather than single words while you read.

Use a guide. Your eyes are designed to follow movement, so a thin pencil underneath the lines you are reading, moved smoothly along, will 'pull' your eyes to faster speeds.

5 And finally...

Have fun while you learn – studies show that those people who enjoy what they are doing understand and remember it more, and generally do it better.

Use your teachers as resource centres. Ask them for help with specific topics and with more general advice on how you can improve your all-round performance.

Personalise your Revision Rescue by underlining and highlighting, by adding notes and pictures. Allow your brain to have a conversation with it!

Tony Buzan

How to use this book

Revision Rescue: Physics for Double Science is clearly divided into subject chapters and topic sections. Each contains the facts you need to know, with key words highlighted for extra clarity.

The tinted boxes contain useful tips and hints, words and ideas to remember and short quizzes to test your knowledge and highlight areas that you may need to revise again.

Each chapter ends with a longer quiz related to the topic covered.

The Exam Emergency Service on Teletext

As you revise, you can boost your knowledge even further with a free exam emergency service on Teletext.

At key revision times, this service offers subject-specific advice, tips and hints for effective exam performance and guidance for planning you revision... until the very last minute! You will find a wide range of subject quizzes, which change regularly so you can test your knowledge again and again.

Living things and the environment 1

Characteristics of life

The characteristics of life are the features that are common to all living things:

- **M**ovement – animals move from place to place because of the action of muscles which pull on the **skeleton**; plants do not usually move from place to place – they move mainly by growing
- **R**espiration occurs in cells and releases energy from food for life's activities; **aerobic** respiration uses oxygen to release energy from food; **anaerobic** respiration releases energy from food without using oxygen
- **S**ensitivity allows living things to detect changes (**stimuli**) in their surroundings and take appropriate action (**response**)
- **G**rowth leads to an increase in size
- **R**eproduction produces new individuals
- **E**xcretion removes the waste substances produced by the chemical reactions (called **metabolism**) taking place in cells
- **N**utrition makes food (by the process of **photosynthesis**) or takes in food for use in the body.

> **Remembering** the mnemonic **MRS GREN** will help you recall the characteristics of life.

Life on Earth

Why can planet Earth support life? Because Earth is:

- close enough to the Sun for its surface temperature to be in the range in which life can exist (an average of 15°C)
- massive enough to have sufficient gravity to hold down an atmosphere of different gases essential for living organisms
- surrounded by a layer of ozone which stops too much ultraviolet light reaching the surface – excess ultraviolet light destroys living things.

Soil, **air** and **water** form Earth's environment.

Earth's physical environment

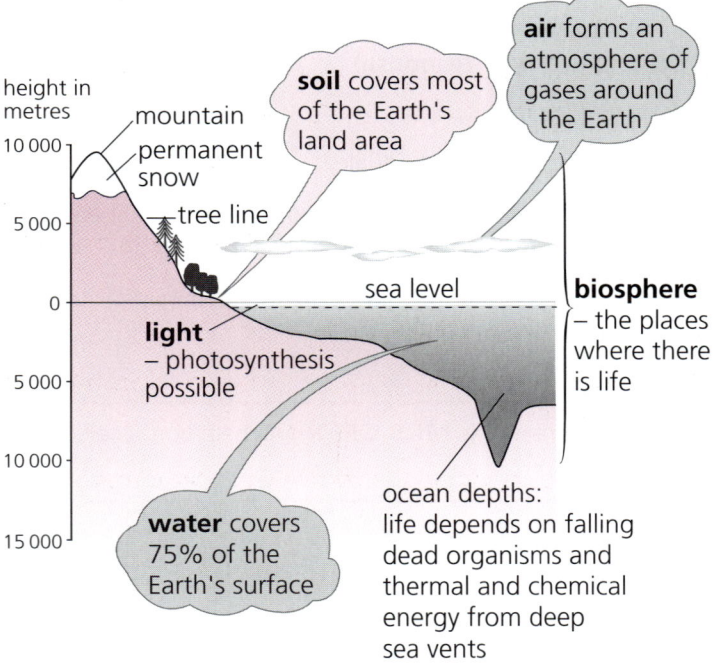

Factfile

Millions of different kinds of organisms live on Earth. It seems likely that life does not exist on other planets in the solar system. Is there life on planets in distant parts of the universe? Probably!

Classification

Organising living things into groups is called **classification**. Some characteristics are unique to the group, other characteristics are shared with other groups. Groups, therefore, combine to form larger groups. The largest group of all is the **kingdom**. Each:

- kingdom contains a number of **phyla**
- phyl**um** (singular) contains a number of **classes**
- class contains a number of **families**
- family contains a number of **genera**
- gen**us** (singular) contains one or more **species**.

The genus and the species identify the individual living thing. For example, humans belong to the genus *Homo* and have the species name *sapiens*. The method of naming living things in two parts is called the **binomial system**. There are **five kingdoms**:

- **Kingdom Plants** – organisms made of many cells – each cell is surrounded by a wall made of cellulose; food is produced by photosynthesis.
- **Kingdom Animals** – organisms made of many cells; food is taken in and usually digested inside the body.
- **Kingdom Fungi** – organisms made of many cells that form thread-like structures called hyphae.
- **Kingdom Protists** – single-celled organisms.
- **Kingdom Bacteria** – single-celled organisms – the cell body is simple in structure compared with protists.

Viruses are sub-microscopic particles – it is difficult to say if they are alive or not.

Quick summary

Remember that each kingdom represents a way of life shared by all its members.

Identifying living things

A **key** is a means of identifying an unfamiliar organism from a selection of specimens. It consists of a set of descriptions. Each description is a clue that helps in the identification. A set of clues makes the key.

The easiest type of key to use is called a **dichotomous** key ('dichotomous' means branching into two). Each time the key branches, you have to choose between two statements. These may be presented diagrammatically as a chart, or written in pairs or **couplets**. By comparing the pairs of statements with the specimen, you will eventually find a description that fits. This identifies the organism. A key is therefore a route to a name. Different keys are used to name different living things. For example:

Identifying different fruits

1 Hairy skin? – GOOSEBERRY.

   Non-hairy skin? – go to 2.

2 Pips on the fruit's surface? – STRAWBERRY.

   No pips on the fruit's surface? – go to 3.

3 Nearly spherical in shape? – go to 4.

   Other shape? – BANANA.

4 Smooth surface? – APPLE.

   Rough surface? – go to 5.

5 Fruit made up of sub-units? – BLACKBERRY.

   Fruit made up of one unit? – ORANGE.

Quick summary

A **key** in biology is a guide to a name. Different keys are used to name different living things.

Looking at an ecosystem

Ecology involves studying relationships between organisms and between organisms and the environment. Organisms and environment together form an **ecosystem**. The organisms are the living – **biotic** – part of the ecosystem forming its **community**. The environment is the non-living – **abiotic** – part, consisting of air, soil and/or water. The relationship between the term ecosystem and other ecological terms is shown below.

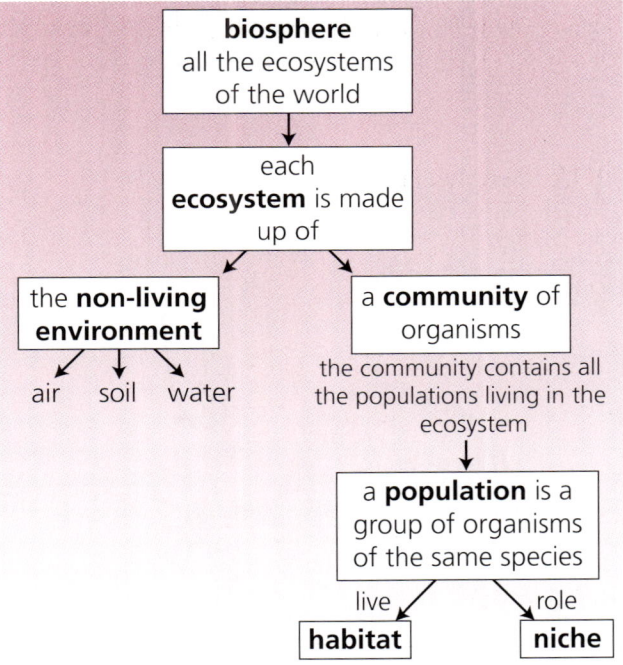

Clear thinking

Think about the relationship between the meaning of the words 'population' and 'species'.

A **population** is a group of individuals of the same species.

A **species** is a group of individuals able to mate and reproduce offspring which themselves are able to mate and reproduce.

It follows that:

A population is a group of individuals able to mate and reproduce fertile offspring.

An oak wood ecosystem

Physical environment
There may be up to 90% less light inside the wood than outside when the canopy is fully developed

The ecosystem

Habitats
canopy layer
shrub layer
field layer
ground layer
detritus layer

Community
1 oak tree
2 holly
3 pigeons, rooks living in canopy
4 toadstools on rotting log

Example habitat
Notice the **decomposers** (which break down dead organic matter) at work on dead wood

- Fungi and bacteria feed on the dead wood causing **decomposition**

★ As a result gases and minerals are released into the environment.

The release of gases and minerals into the soil through decomposition represents the **niche** of fungi and bacteria.

Food chains

Plants, algae and some bacteria are called **producers** because they use sunlight to produce food by **photosynthesis**. Animals do not produce food. They are called **consumers** because they eat food.

- **Herbivores** eat plants.
- **Carnivores** eat meat.
- **Omnivores** eat both plants and meat.

Predators catch and eat other animals. **Prey** are the animals that are caught. **Scavengers** are carnivores that feed on dead bodies.

A **food chain** shows the links between plants, prey, predators and scavengers (see figure).

Food chain in an oak wood

Note

- The arrows represent the transfer of food between different organisms
- the arrows point from the eaten to the eater
- the number of links in a food chain is usually four or less.

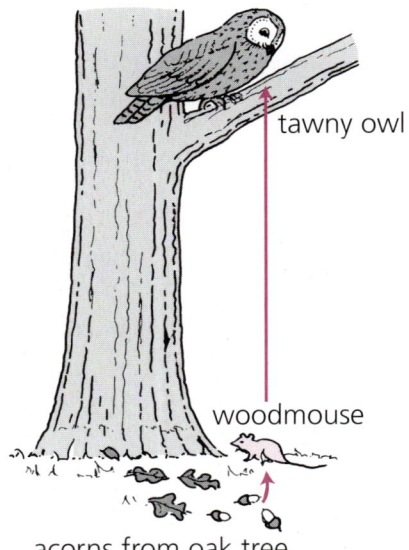

tawny owl

woodmouse

acorns from oak tree

Extra tips

A **food chain** represents *one* pathway of **food energy** through the community.

Food webs

Most animals eat more than one type of plant or other animal. The feeding relationships are shown as a **food web** (see figure below).

Note

- Several food chains link up to form a food web
- different types of animal may eat the same type of food.

A food web is usually a more accurate description of feeding relationships in a community than a food chain. Why? – Because a food web shows all the feeding links between plants, prey, predators and scavengers.

Food web in an oak wood

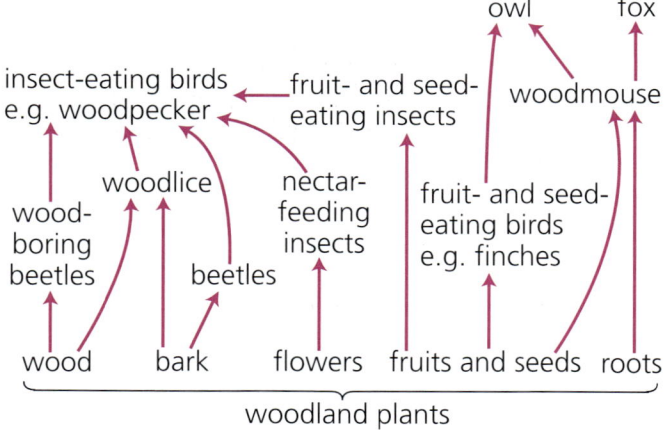

Remember

Food chains and food webs begin with producers. Why? – Because producers can use sunlight to produce food by photosynthesis.

Extra tips

A **food web** represents *many* pathways of **food energy** through the community.

Ecological pyramids

Remember

Many plants support a limited number of herbivores which in turn support fewer carnivores. Food chains and food webs do not tell us about the number of individuals involved. **Ecological pyramids** do!

Pyramid of numbers for a grassland community in 0.1 hectare

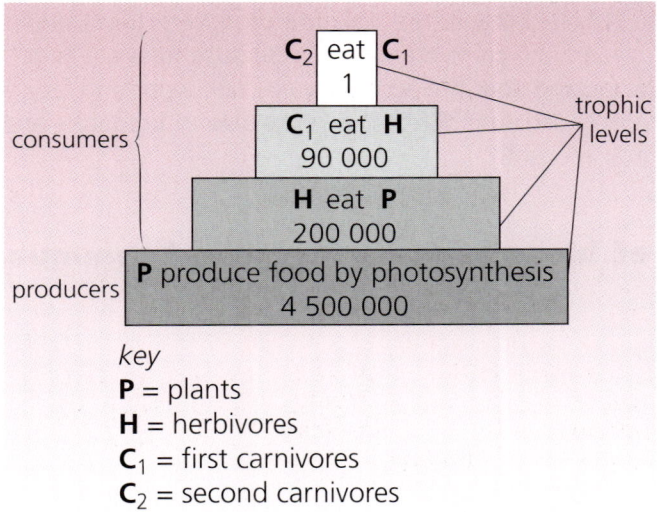

key
P = plants
H = herbivores
C_1 = first carnivores
C_2 = second carnivores

Note

The **pyramid of numbers** for a grassland community has several feeding levels called **trophic levels** (all ecological pyramids are built of trophic levels).

Each trophic level groups together organisms that have similar types of food. Pyramids of numbers show the numbers of organisms in each trophic level at a particular moment in time.

Factfile

Snails and cows are **herbivores**. They belong to the *same* **trophic level**.

Pyramid of numbers for a woodland community

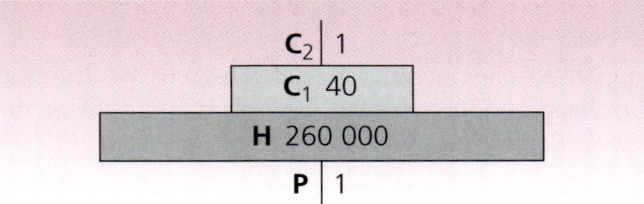

Note

The pyramid of numbers for a woodland community has a point at the bottom as well as the top. Why? – Because relatively few producers (trees) support a large number of herbivores and carnivores. Why? – Because trees are large! A numbers pyramid for a woodland does not accurately describe woodland feeding relationships. Why? – Because differences in the **size** of producers and consumers are not taken into account.

Pyramid of biomass for a woodland community

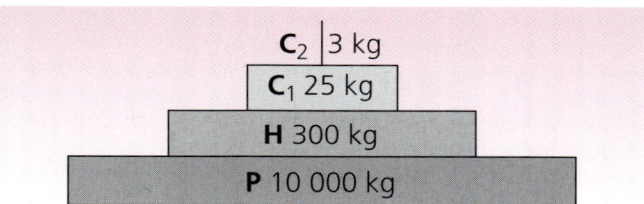

A **pyramid of biomass** allows for differences in the size of organisms. Why? – Because the pyramid shows the **amount of organic material** (as dry mass) in each trophic level at a particular moment in time.

Quick quiz

Why is **dry** mass used to plot **pyramids of biomass**?

Answer

Dry mass is used because **fresh** mass **varies** greatly as organisms contain different amounts of **water**.

Pyramid of energy for a stream (in kJ/m²/year)

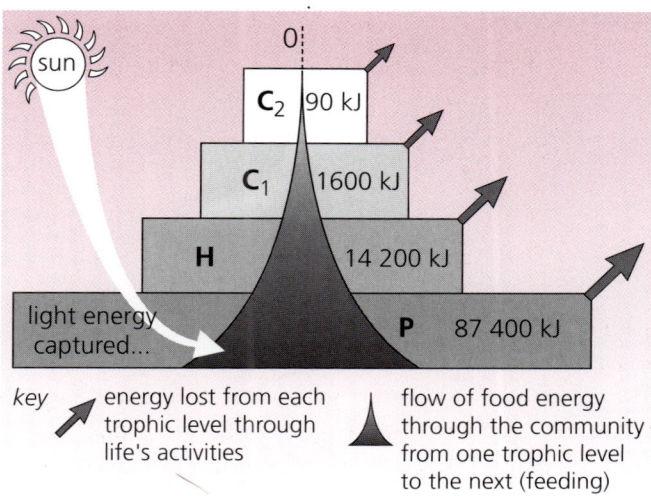

A **pyramid of energy** shows energy flow through, and energy loss from, a community over a period of time. Its shape therefore is not affected by differences in size.

Note

- Feeding transfers food energy from one trophic level to the next
- energy is lost from each trophic level – mostly as heat released by the metabolism of cells
  - ★ as a result the amount of food energy in a trophic level is less than the one below it
  - ★ as a result the amount of living material (biomass) in a trophic level is less than the one below it.

Now you know why there is a limited number of links in a food chain (see page 13).

Factfile

The energy pyramid shows the **amount of food** being **produced** and **consumed** over a period of **time**.

See also • p.7 **Metabolism**

Decomposition and cycles

The nitrogen cycle

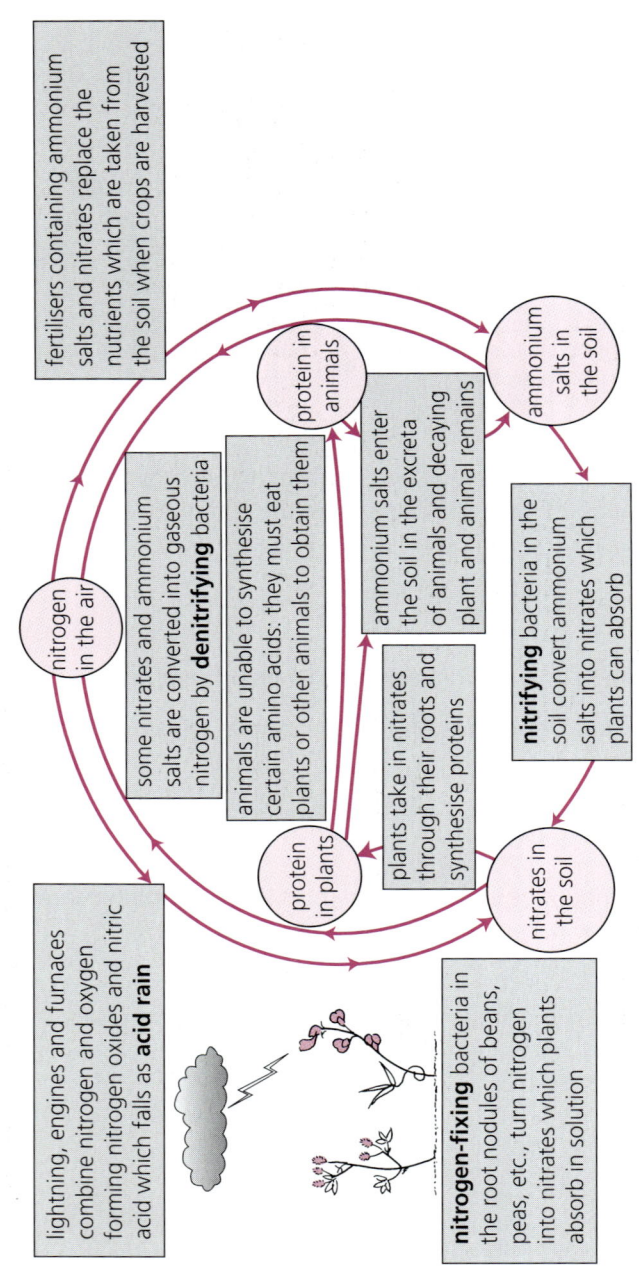

Nitrogen circulates from air to soil to living things and back again in the nitrogen cycle

The carbon cycle

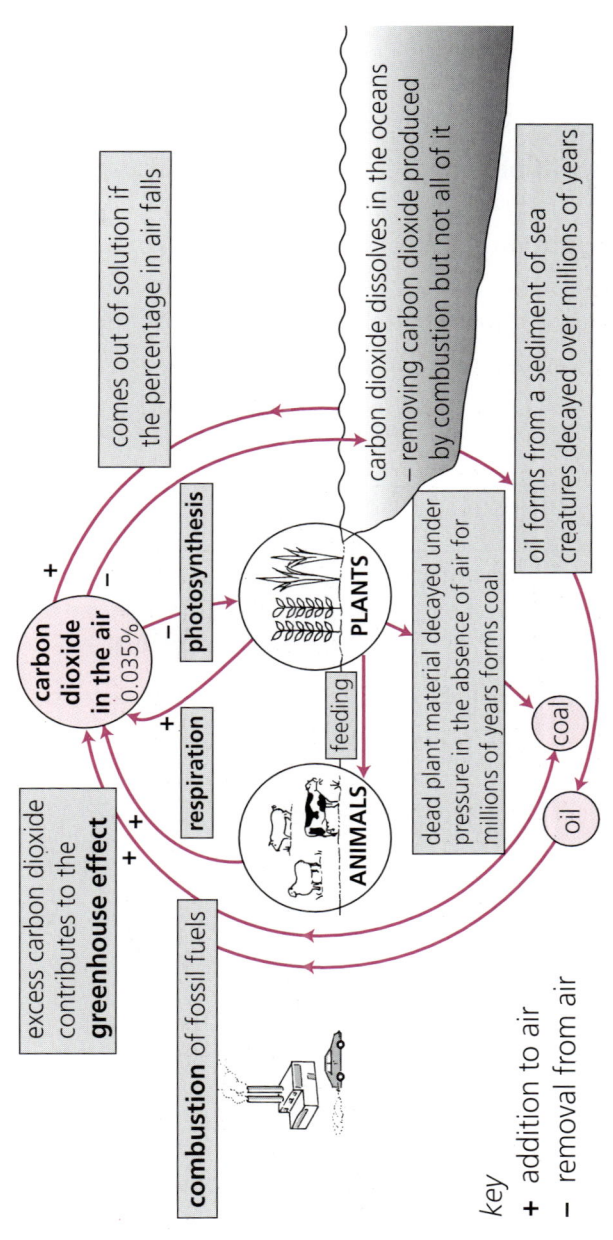

The carbon cycle shows those processes that put carbon dioxide into the air and those that remove carbon dioxide from the air

See also • p.24 **Greenhouse effect** • p.39 **Photosynthesis** • p.59 **Respiration**

Distribution of organisms

Different factors affect the **distribution** of organisms. Physical factors include:

- the amount of light
- the abundance of water.

Biological factors include:

- **intraspecific competition** – competition between individuals of the same species
- **interspecific competition** – competition between individuals of different species
- **adaptations** of organisms for survival in different environments
- **interactions** between predators and prey.

Predators are adapted to catch prey, and prey are adapted to escape predators:

Predator	Prey
Catches a variety of species, reducing the risk of starvation should a prey species decline in numbers	Large groups (e.g. herds) distract predators from concentrating on a particular individual
Catches young, old and sick prey	Stings and bitter tastes deter predators
Catches large prey which provide more food per kill	Warning coloration tells predators to avoid particular prey
Moves to areas where prey is plentiful	Shock tactics startle predators
Camouflage allows predator to 'surprise' prey	Camouflage conceals prey
	Prey tries to run/swim/fly faster than predator

Remember

Rivals for something in short supply (e.g. water, light, space) are **competitors**.

Remember

Organisms are **adapted** (suited) for the environment in which they live and for their role (niche) in that environment.

Population size

Limiting factors which slow down population growth include: **shortages of** food, oxygen, water, light and shelter **and build up of** poisonous wastes, predators, parasites, disease and social factors.

Population growth curve

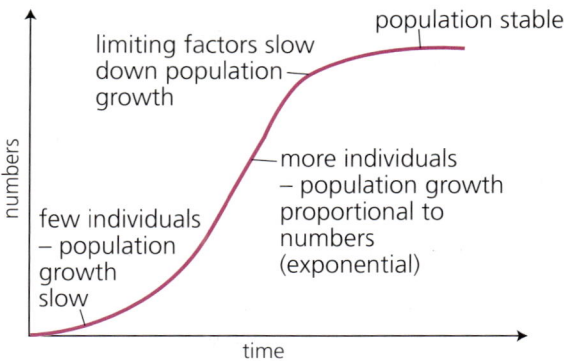

Predator – prey relationships

A predator and its prey affect the size of the other's population.

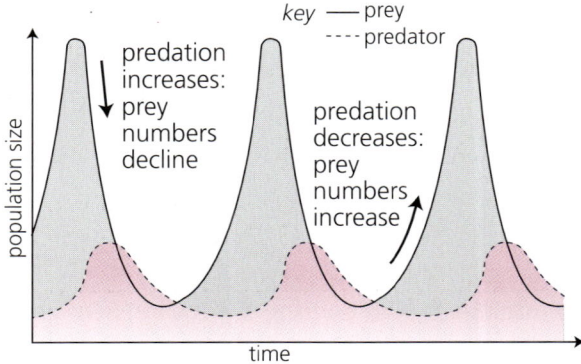

Improvements in food production, medical care and public health have led to an **increase** in the human population. Better contraception, economic development and the changing role of women in society **all** help to **slow** growth.

See also • p. 11 **Population**

Producing food

The amount of food a farm produces depends on:
- the amount of energy entering the farm ecosystem
- the efficiency with which the energy is converted into plant and animal tissue.

Remember

The **fewer** the links in a food chain, the **less** food energy is lost and so the **more** food is available to consumers. Energy transfer between producers and consumers is inefficient because:
- undigested plant material passes out of the herbivore body as faeces
- the herbivore uses energy to stay alive.

Therefore eating meat is wasteful in terms of food energy.

Intensive farming

Intensive farming methods are used to produce as much food as possible from the land available:
- **monoculture** – where a single crop is grown over a large area
- **artificial fertilisers** supply nutrients directly to crops
- **irrigation** brings water to land that would otherwise be too dry to grow crops
- **mechanisation** – farm machinery works best in large, open fields – fuel oil powers the machinery
- use of **pesticides**: **insecticides** kill insects, **herbicides** kill weeds, **fungicides** kill fungi.

Factfile

Producing **food intensively** can damage the environment and give rise to risks to public health:
- monoculture reduces the diversity of wildlife
- irrigation increases the concentration of mineral salts in the soil, making land too 'salty' to grow crops
- mechanisation leads to the destruction of habitats as land is cleared to make fields larger.

See also • p. 13 **Food chains** • p. 17 **Pyramid of energy** • p. 43 **Plant nutrients**

Pollution

Pollution is caused by **industry** making goods that maintain our standard of living and **intensive farming** that produces large quantities of food. **Acid rain** (pH 2.4–5.0) results from industrial processes releasing gases which react with water vapour and oxygen in the air:

- **sulphur dioxide** forms sulphuric acid (H_2SO_4)
- **oxides of nitrogen** form nitric acid (HNO_3)
    - ★ as a result mineral salts (nutrients) needed for healthy plant growth are removed – **leached** – from the soil
    - ★ as a result acid rain enters rivers and lakes killing wildlife.

Using low-sulphur fuels and removing sulphur dioxide from the waste gases leaving chimneys helps to reduce the amount of sulphur dioxide entering the atmosphere. The **ozone layer** – 5 km thick – surrounds the Earth at a distance of 25–30 km from the Earth's surface. It cuts out some of the Sun's ultraviolet light which would otherwise be harmful to life but there are gaps in the layer now. Ozone oxidises pollutants that accumulate in the upper atmosphere.

- **Chlorofluorocarbons** (CFCs) which are aerosol **propellants** react with ozone producing oxygen.
- **Nitrogen monoxide** coming from the exhausts of high altitude aircraft reacts with oxygen to form nitrogen dioxide.

The use of CFCs is being reduced.

Exam tips

Land use destroys habitats reducing the variety of wildlife. The pressures are:
- economic development
- growing human populations
- the increasing need for food to feed people.

Quick quiz

Why are chemists in a hurry to develop **substitutes** for **chlorofluorocarbons**?

Answer

To **prevent** further **damage** to the **ozone layer**.

See also • p. 13 **Food chains** • p. 39 **Photosynthesis** • p. 60 **Haemoglobin**

Carbon dioxide and water vapour in the atmosphere warm the Earth's surface naturally – the **greenhouse effect**. However, the Earth's surface has warmed up by 0.75°C during the last one hundred years. Why?

- Burning **fossil fuels** releases carbon dioxide into the air.
- **Clear felling** tropical rain forests reduces the amount of vegetation taking carbon dioxide from the air for **photosynthesis**.
- Increasing rice cultivation and numbers of livestock releases large volumes of **methane** (another greenhouse gas) into the air.

Warming of the Earth's surface will probably increase the rate of **melting** of the polar ice caps:

★ as a result sea levels will rise
★ as a result coastal areas will be flooded.

Nitrate fertilisers – excess contaminates water:

- fertilisation of the water increases the rate of growth of algae; when the algae die, bacteria decompose the dead material using up available oxygen (increasing **Biological Oxygen Demand**), so killing wildlife
- nitrates are converted into **nitrites** – which the body converts into **nitrosamines** – a cause of cancer. **Also** in babies, nitrites reduce the ability of haemoglobin to combine with oxygen.

Pesticides kill wildlife. Some insecticides (e.g. DDT, dieldrin) persist in the environment, **accumulate** in food chains and may cause illness in humans. In the USA and Europe, the use of DDT is now **banned**.

Factfile

Pesticides are chemicals which kill **pests** that damage **crops**:
- **insecticides** kill insects
- **herbicides** kill weeds (unwanted plants)
- **fungicides** kill fungi
- **molluscicides** kill slugs and snails.

Living things and the environment quiz

Questions

1 List the different components of an ecosystem.

2 Briefly describe how a biological key is used.

3 In the 1890s, when people saw cars for the first time, many thought that the cars were alive. Imagine that you are a reporter writing a short article for the local newspaper reassuring the populace that although cars seem to move under their own steam, they are not alive.

4 (a) Why is a food web a more accurate description of feeding in a community than a food chain?

(b) Why do food chains and food webs always begin with plants?

5 Give reasons for the rapid increase in human population.

Answers

1 physical or abiotic environment / living or biotic community / habitats / niches

2 the unfamiliar specimen is compared against the descriptions in the key until the description that matches the specimen is found; this identifies the specimen

3 although cars move; need fuel (= nutrition); burn fuel (= respiration); and produce waste gases (= excretion); they do not grow or reproduce and are not sensitive. Cars therefore do not show all the characteristics associated with living things

4 (a) most animals eat more than one type of plant or other animal / a food web shows the range of different food eaten (b) plants produce food by photosynthesis / animals consume this food directly when they eat plants or indirectly when they eat other animals which depend on plant food

5 improvements in food production; more jobs; new drugs (accept improvement in medicines/medical care); improvement in public health

Cells 2

Cell structure

Microscopes help us see cells

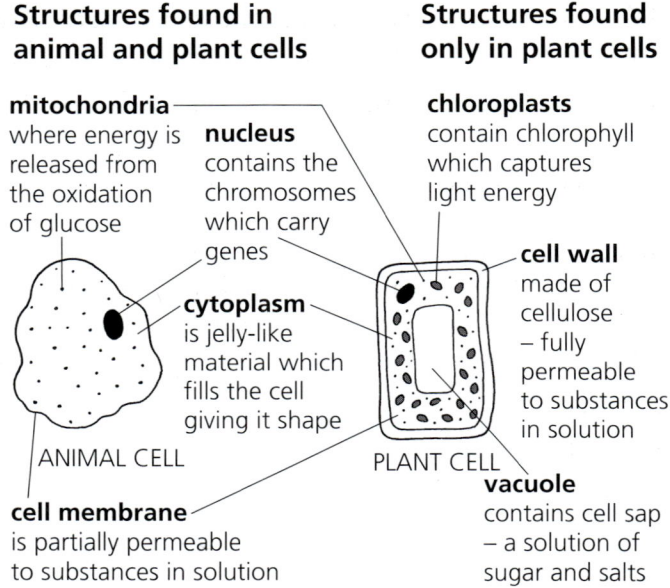

More than 200 different types of cell make up the human body. Fewer types of cell make up the plant body. Each type of cell is suited (**adapted**) for its particular **function** (the way it works). For example:

- **sperm cells** each have a tail-like flagellum that helps the sperm swim to an egg
- **red blood cells** transport oxygen around the body
- **leaf palisade cells** each contain chloroplasts packed with chlorophyll which absorbs light.

Exam tips

Remember which **structures** are found in animal cells *and* plant cells, and in plant cells *only*.

Molecules on the move

Substances move inside, and into and out of cells (see figure on page 28).

Diffusion: the movement of a substance through a solution or gas **down** a **concentration gradient** (that is, from a region of high concentration of the substance to a region of low concentration). The steeper the concentration gradient, the faster the substance diffuses.

Active transport: the movement of a substance through a solution **up** (against) a concentration gradient (that is, from a region of low concentration of the substance to a region of high concentration).

- Cells may build up **stores** of a substance which would otherwise be spread out by diffusion.
- Active transport requires more energy than diffusion.

Osmosis: the movement of **water down** a concentration gradient through a partially permeable membrane. A **partially permeable** membrane allows some substances to pass through but stops others. The passage of substances across such a membrane depends on the:

- size of the molecules
- size of the membrane pores
- surface area of the membrane
- rate of diffusion.

Factfile

Understanding **water potential** will help you think about **osmosis** in a different way.

Water potential is a measure of the tendency of water to *leave* a solution. Osmosis occurs when there is a net movement of water molecules through a **partially permeable membrane** from a region of *high* water potential to a region of *low* water potential.

Diffusion, active transport and osmosis

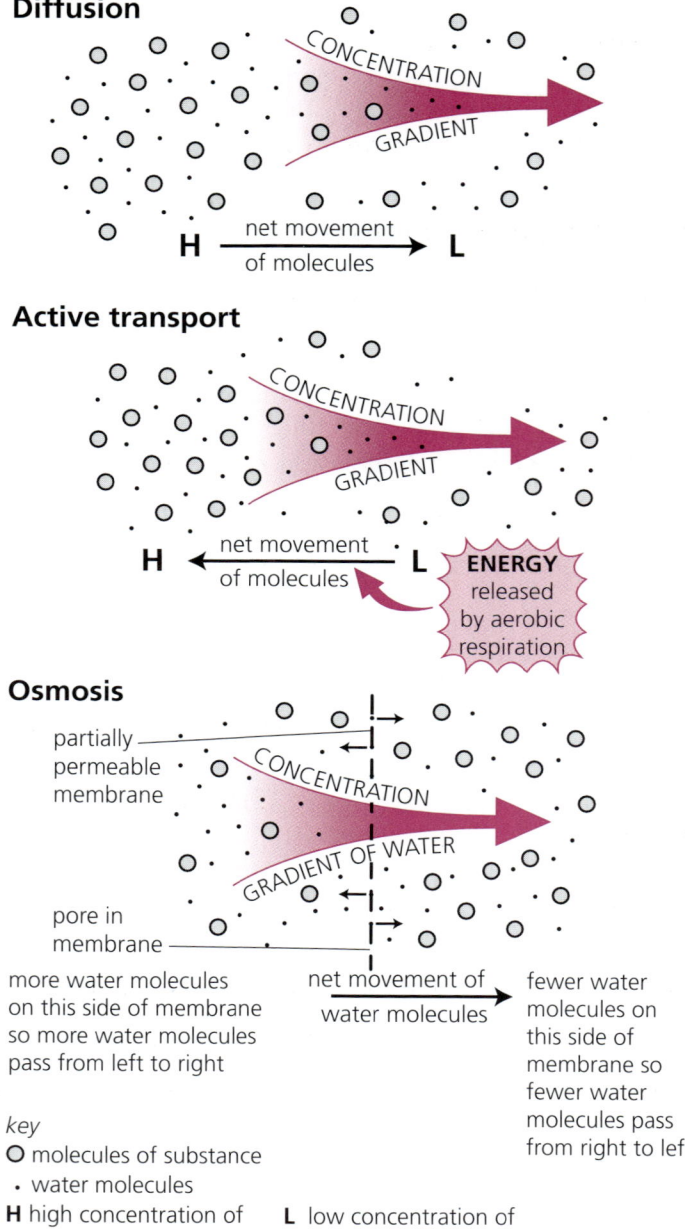

Cells, tissues and organs

Plants and animals are made of many types of cells – they are **multicellular**.

- A group of similar cells makes a **tissue**.
- Different tissues together make up an **organ**.
- Different organs combine to make an **organ system**.

Surface area to volume ratio

All cells **exchange** materials with their environment.

Remember

As a cell grows its:

- surface area (SA) increases with the square (power^2) of the side
- volume (V) increases with the cube (power^3) of the side
  - ★ as a result, the larger the cell becomes, the smaller its surface area to volume ratio (SA/V)
- after a cell reaches a certain size its surface area becomes too small to meet the needs of the larger volume of living matter inside
- at this point the cell divides into two smaller daughter cells, each with a larger SA/V than the parent cell
  - ★ as a result the cells can exchange sufficient material between themselves and the environment.

Different organs and organ systems are specialised to make the SA/V as large as possible:

- **villi** increase the SA of the gut wall for the absorption of food
- **alveoli** increase the SA of the lungs for the diffusion of gases
- **root branches** and **root hairs** increase the SA for the absorption of water.

Exam tips

Remember that the *larger* the cell, the *smaller* is its surface area to volume ratio.

See also • p. 42 **Roots** • p. 53 **Villi** • p. 57 **Alveoli**

Cell division

Cells divide in one of two ways (see the figure on page 31):

Mitosis produces new (**daughter**) cells with the same number of chromosomes as the parent cell. The daughter cells are described as **diploid** (or **2n**). The **cells of the body** – except the cells of the sex organs which give rise to the sex cells (**gametes**) – divide by mitosis.

Meiosis produces daughter cells each with only half the number of chromosomes of the parent cell. The daughter cells are described as **haploid** (or **n**). **Sex cells** (sperms and eggs) are produced by meiosis.

The importance of mitosis

The daughter cells each receive an identical **full** (diploid) set of chromosomes from the parent cell. As a result:

★ the parent cell and its daughter cells are genetically identical – they form a **clone**
★ mitosis is the way in which living things repair damage; grow; reproduce asexually.

The importance of meiosis

The daughter cells each receive a **half** (haploid) set of chromosomes from the parent cell. As a result:

★ during fertilisation the chromosomes from the sperm and egg combine
★ the fertilised egg – **zygote** – is diploid but inherits a new combination of genes contributed (50:50) from the parents
★ the new individual inherits characteristics from both parents.

Quick quiz

Which type of **cell division** occurs to **repair** the skin if it is cut?

Answer: Mitosis

See also • p. 83 **Sex cells** and **Reproduction**

Mitosis and meiosis – sequence of events

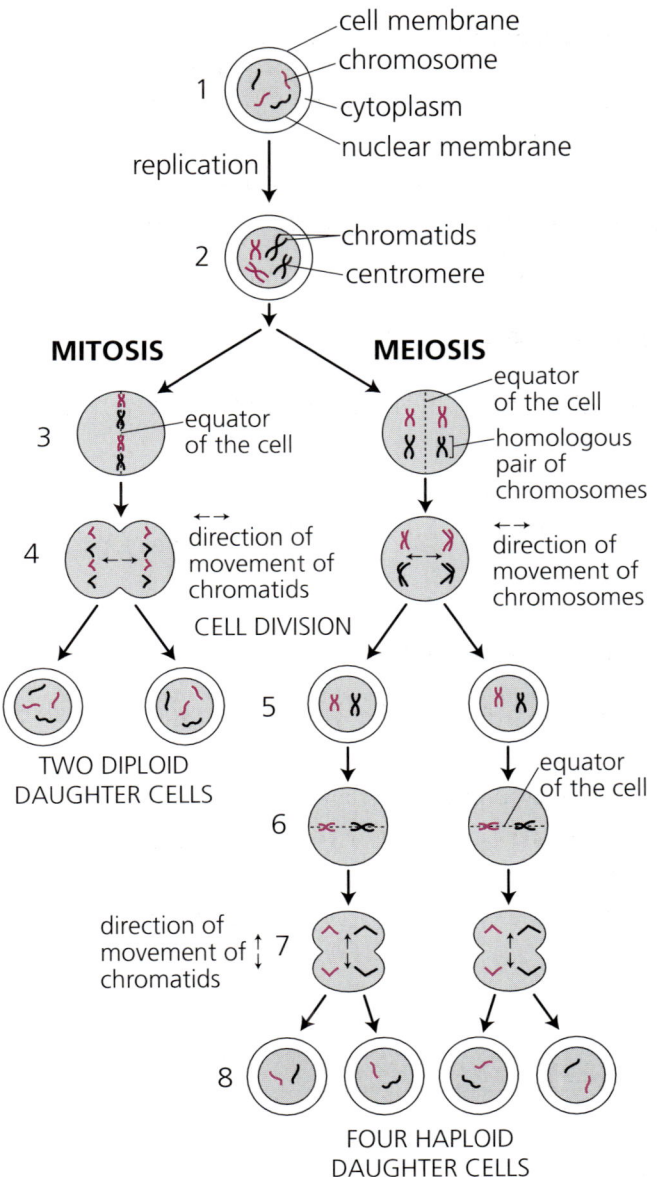

Comparing mitosis and meiosis

Mitosis	Meiosis
1 The chromosomes shorten, fatten and become visible under a microscope	1 The chromosomes shorten, fatten and become visible under a microscope
2 Each chromosome divides into a pair of identical (replica) chromatids joined to one another by the centromere	2 Each chromosome divides into a pair of identical (replica) chromatids joined to one another by the centromere
3 The chromatids line up on the equator (middle) of the cell – the nuclear membrane has disappeared	3 Matching chromosomes form homologous pairs and line up on the equator (middle) of the cell – the nuclear membrane disappears
4 The chromatids separate and move to the opposite ends of the cell, which begins to divide	4 Homologous pairs of chromosomes separate
5 The chromatids are now the new chromosomes of the two daughter cells – a nuclear membrane forms around each group of chromosomes.	5 A new nuclear membrane forms around each group of chromosomes – the cell divides
	6 The nuclear membrane disappears – the chromosomes (still as pairs of chromatids) arrange themselves on the equator (middle) of the cell
	7 The chromatids separate, they are now the new chromosomes – each cell begins to divide
	8 Cell division occurs and a nuclear membrane forms around each group of chromosomes.

Chemicals in living things – carbohydrates

The mnemonic **CHNOPS** helps you remember important elements in order of their abundance in living matter.

- carbon (C)
- hydrogen (H)
- nitrogen (N)
- oxygen (O)
- phosphorus (P)
- sulphur (S)

Carbohydrates contain carbon, hydrogen and oxygen. They are a source of energy and structural materials. There are three categories:

Monosaccharides are simple sugars. Sweet-tasting **fructose** and **glucose** are examples – both have the molecular formula $C_6H_{12}O_6$ but different structural formulas.

Disaccharides are complex sugars. They are formed when two monosaccharides combine. For example:

2 glucose → maltose + water

$2 C_6H_{12}O_6 \rightarrow C_{12}H_{22}O_{11}$ (aq) $+ H_2O$

 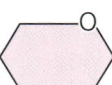

fructose   glucose

Polysaccharides are formed from hundreds of sugar rings joined together:

- **starch** is a food substance stored in plants
- **glycogen** is a food substance stored in animals
- **cellulose** is a component of the cell walls of plants
- **chitin** is a component of the exoskeleton of insects.

Part of a starch molecule

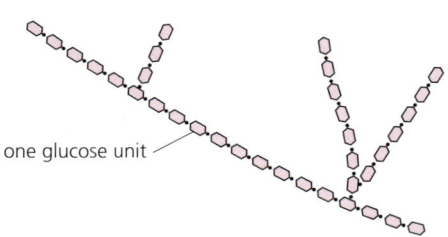

one glucose unit

Exam tips

Remember that **starch** and **glycogen** are **food** substances which are **sources** of **stored energy**. **Cellulose** and **chitin** are **structural** materials.

Lipids and proteins

Lipids contain carbon, hydrogen and oxygen. **Fats** are solid at room temperature and **oils** are liquid at room temperature.

A **triglyceride** forms as follows:

glycerol + fatty acid → triglyceride + water

$$\begin{array}{l} \text{-OH} \\ \text{-OH} \\ \text{-OH} \end{array} + 3\text{HA} \longrightarrow \begin{array}{l} \text{-A} \\ \text{-A} \\ \text{-A} \end{array} + 3H_2O$$

Lipids are a mixture of triglycerides.

Saturated fats form from fatty acids in which the carbon atoms are joined by **single** bonds.

Unsaturated fats form from fatty acids in which the carbon atoms have **double** bonds between them. Fats and oils are important as:

- components of cell membranes
- sources of energy
- sources of fat-soluble vitamins A, D and E
- insulation which helps keep the body warm
- protection for delicate organs.

Proteins contain carbon, hydrogen, oxygen, nitrogen and sometimes sulphur.

Amino acids combine to make **peptides** and proteins – there are about 20 different amino acids.

Proteins are the materials from which new tissues are made during **growth** and **repair**.

- **Enzymes** are proteins which control the rates of chemical reactions in cells – **metabolism**.
- **Hormones** are proteins which control the activities of organisms.

Nucleic acids

Lengths of **deoxyribonucleic acid** (**DNA**) form the **genes** that carry information from parents to offspring. They carry the **genetic code** which tells cells how to assemble amino acids in the correct order to make proteins.

Ribonucleic acid (**RNA**) transfers the information in genes to the places in the cell where proteins are made. DNA and RNA are made from smaller molecules called **nucleotides**.

- Each nucleotide consists of sugar – deoxyribose in DNA; ribose in RNA; phosphate and a base – one of either **adenine** (A), **cytosine** (C), **guanine** (G) or **thymine** (T); in RNA **uracil** (U) replaces (T).
- Many nucleotides join together to form a strand of DNA (or RNA).
- When two strands link together by **base pairing** (always A pairs with T and G pairs with C) and twist into a spiral, a **double helix** forms.

The double helix: two spiral strands connected by their bases

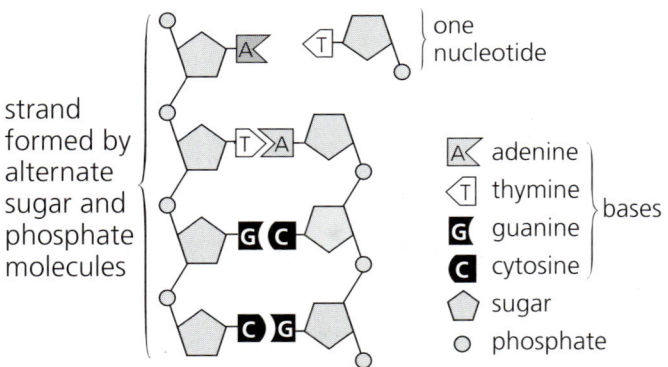

Quick quiz

What is a **nucleotide**?

Answer

A nucleotide consists of the sugar ribose or deoxyribose, one of five different bases and a phosphate group.

Enzymes in action

Enzymes are proteins made by living cells. They are catalysts which control the speed of chemical reactions in cells. Enzymes are:

- **specific** in their action – each enzyme catalyses a certain chemical reaction or type of chemical reaction
- sensitive to changes in **pH**
- sensitive to changes in **temperature**.

The substance that the enzyme helps to react is called the **substrate**. The substances formed in the reaction are called **products**.

The features of enzymes are shown on page 37.

Enzymes also speed up the **digestion** of food in the **gut**. They catalyse the breakdown of food by **hydrolysis**. Water splits large molecules of food into smaller molecules which are suitable for **absorption** into the body. Enzymes are useful **industrial catalysts**.

- Only a particular reaction is catalysed by an enzyme, making it easier to collect and purify the products.
- Enzyme activity is high at moderate temperature and pH.
- Only small amounts of enzyme are required.
- The enzyme is not used up in the reaction.

Enzymes bonded to insoluble supporting materials, **immobilised enzymes**, are:

- easily recovered to re-use
- active at temperatures that would destroy unprotected enzymes
- not diluted and therefore do not contaminate the product.

Factfile

The thousands of chemical reactions (**metabolism**) taking place inside a cell are each controlled by an **enzyme**.

See also • p. 53 **Absorption** • p. 54 **Digestive enzymes**

Enzymes

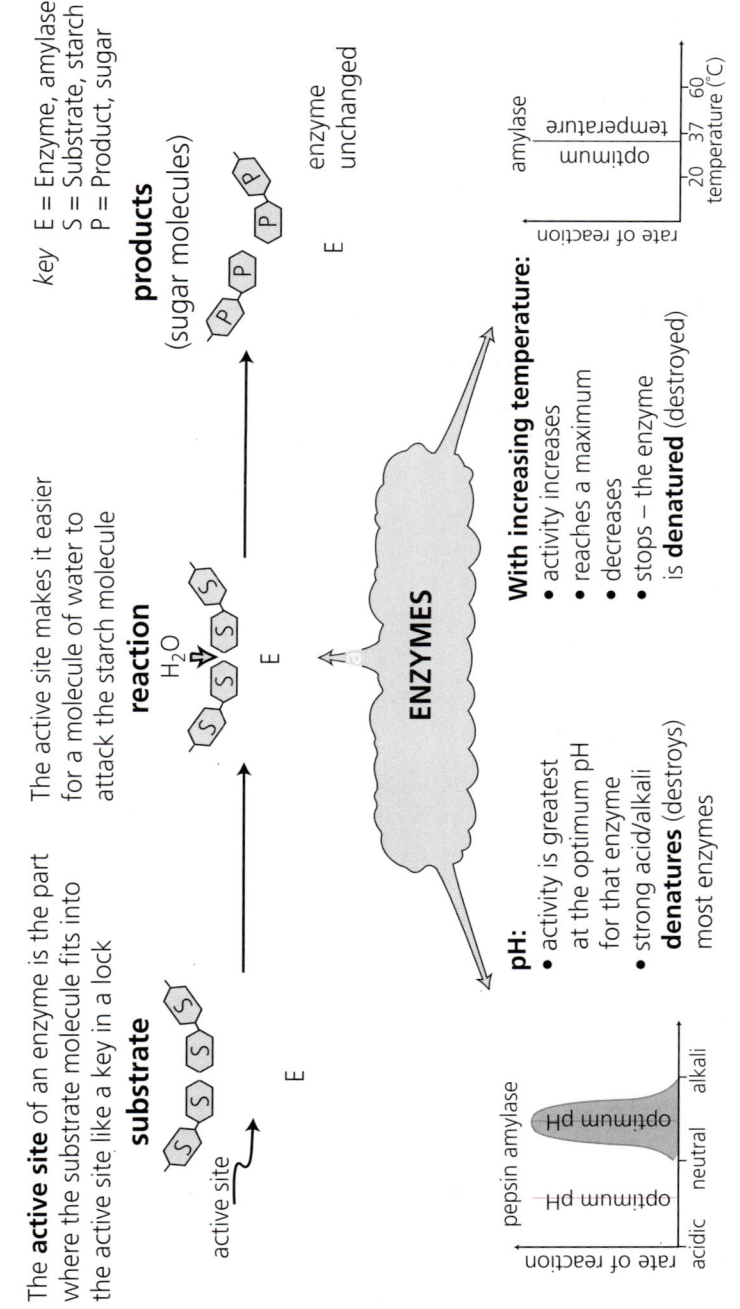

Cells quiz

Questions

1. Which of the structures listed below are found in (a) animal cells and plant cells (b) plant cells only?

   nucleus   cell membrane   cell wall   large vacuole   mitochondria   chloroplasts   cytoplasm

2. Describe what happens in the cells of a plant deprived of water which is then watered.

3. Compare and contrast the processes of mitosis and meiosis by listing the similarities and the differences.

4. Match each substance in column A with its function in column B.

A	B
Fat	Carries the genetic code
Cellulose	Insulates the body
DNA	A food substance stored in the liver
Glycogen	A component of the plant cell wall

Answers

1. **Animal cells and plant cells**: nucleus   mitochondria   cell membrane   cytoplasm
   Plant cells only: cell wall   chloroplasts   large vacuole

2. water is taken into the cells by osmosis / the cells become turgid

3. **similarities** – replication of each chromosome into chromatids / lining up of the chromosomes on the equator of the cell / separation of the chromatids / chromatids are the new chromosomes in daughter cells / destruction and reformation of the nuclear membrane during the process of cell division   **differences** – chromosomes form homologous pairs in meiosis but not mitosis / there are two divisions during meiosis but only one division during mitosis / meiosis results in four daughter cells; mitosis results in two daughter cells

4. | A | B |
   |---|---|
   | fat | insulates the body |
   | cellulose | a component of the plant cell wall |
   | DNA | carries the genetic code |
   | glycogen | a food substance stored in the liver |

Plants as organisms 3

Photosynthesis

Chlorophyll is a green pigment which traps the energy of **sunlight**. The energy powers the chemical reactions of **photosynthesis** inside the **chloroplasts** of the **leaves** and other green parts of the plant.

$$\text{carbon dioxide} + \text{water} \xrightarrow{\text{catalysed by chlorophyll}} \text{sugars} + \text{oxygen}$$
$$6CO_2(g) + 6H_2O(l) \rightarrow C_6H_{12}O_6(aq) + 6O_2(g)$$

Limiting factors affect the rate of photosynthesis:

- **carbon dioxide** at low concentration limits the rate of photosynthesis whatever the light intensity
- **dim light** limits the rate of photosynthesis even if the level of carbon dioxide remains high
- the higher the **temperature** the faster is the rate of photosynthesis – within limits (> 0°C and < 45°C)
- **lack of water** limits metabolism (including photosynthesis) because water is a solvent for chemical reactions.

In a greenhouse conditions are **controlled** so that limiting factors are eliminated.

The maximum-efficiency greenhouse

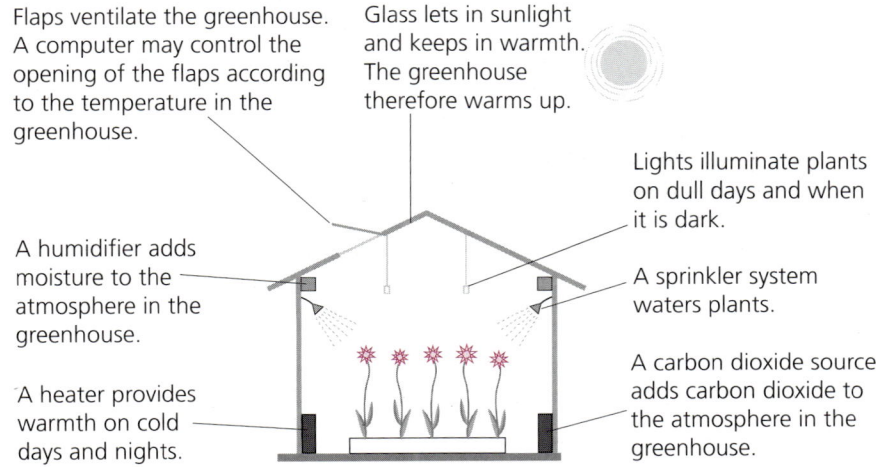

Flaps ventilate the greenhouse. A computer may control the opening of the flaps according to the temperature in the greenhouse.

Glass lets in sunlight and keeps in warmth. The greenhouse therefore warms up.

Lights illuminate plants on dull days and when it is dark.

A humidifier adds moisture to the atmosphere in the greenhouse.

A sprinkler system waters plants.

A heater provides warmth on cold days and nights.

A carbon dioxide source adds carbon dioxide to the atmosphere in the greenhouse.

See also • p. 7 **Metabolism** • p. 26 **Chloroplasts**

Inside the leaf

A leaf is **adapted** for photosynthesis.

- **Palisade cells** packed beneath the transparent epidermis are filled with chloroplasts
    - ★ as a result many chloroplasts are exposed to bright light.
- **Spongy mesophyll cells** are loosely packed
    - ★ as a result there are air spaces between them and carbon dioxide and water vapour circulate freely – bringing the raw materials for photosynthesis to the leaf cells.
- **Guard cells** control the size of the opening of the stoma
    - ★ as a result the rate of diffusion of gases through the stomata is controlled.
- The cells of the lower leaf surface lack chloroplasts, except the guard cells.

Cross-section of a leaf

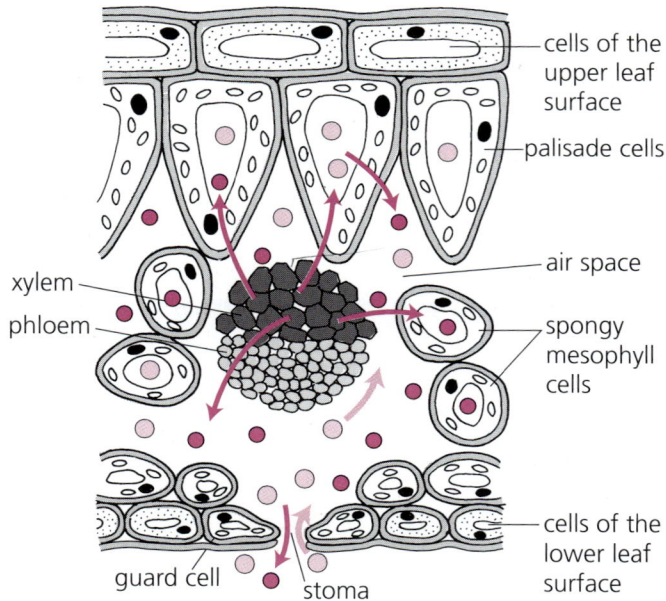

key
- ○ carbon dioxide molecule
- ● water molecule
- → CO₂ diffusion
- → uptake / loss of water

Transport in plants

Xylem tissue transports **water** – **dead** xylem cells form tubes through which water is drawn. The walls of xylem tubes are waterproofed with a substance called **lignin**.

Phloem tissue transports **food** in flowering plants. **Living** phloem consists of tubes of **sieve cells** and **companion cells**.

The arrangement of xylem and phloem in flowering plants

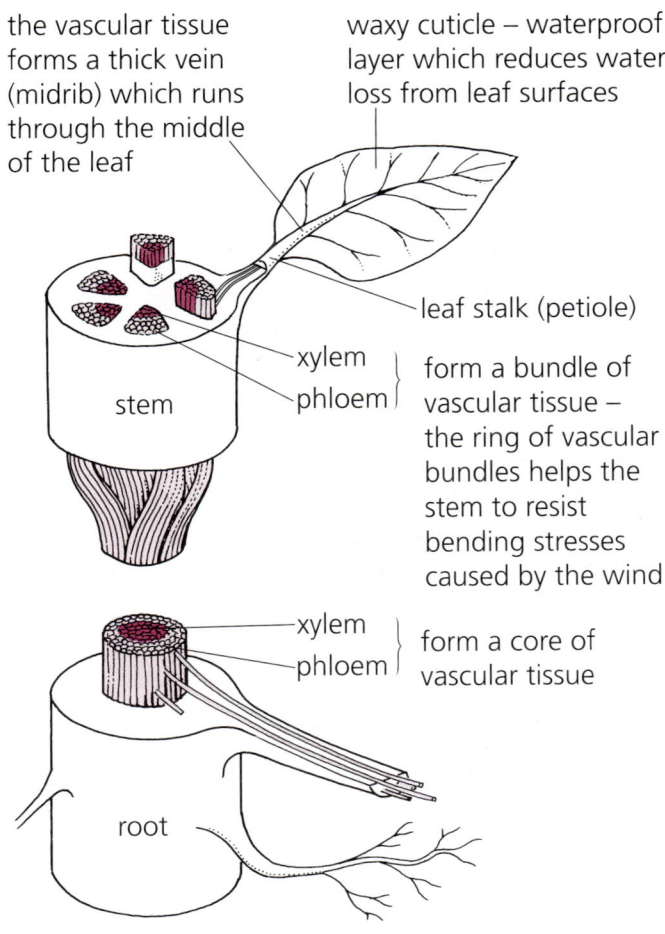

Transport of water and minerals

The movement of water and minerals in solution from the soil and through the plant is shown on page 43.

- Root hairs absorb water from the soil by **osmosis**; mineral ions are **actively transported** into the root.
- Water passes **through** the root tissue into the xylem by **osmosis**.
- Water travels through the xylem of the root and stem in unbroken columns – **the transpiration stream**.
- Water moves through the xylem of the leaf stalk and veins of the leaf.
- Water evaporates into the large air spaces within the leaf – the air spaces are saturated with water vapour.
- The concentration of water vapour in the atmosphere is lower than that in the air spaces – water vapour therefore diffuses from the leaf through the stomata; the process is called **transpiration**.
- Water lost by cells through evaporation is replaced with water drawn through the cells by osmosis – cells next to the xylem draw water from the xylem by osmosis.

Plants **lose** water through transpiration and **gain** water through its uptake by the roots. If the loss of water is **greater** than the gain then the stomata close and transpiration is reduced. If the loss of water continues then the cells of the plant lose **turgor** (ridigity) and the plant **wilts**.

Different factors **increase** the rate of transpiration:

- ↑ temperature
- ↑ wind velocity
- ↓ humidity
- ↑ light intensity.

Exam tips

Remember to make sure that you know the **distribution of chloroplasts** in the different types of cell in the leaf:

palisade cells
spongy mesophyll cells   } have chloroplasts
guard cells

cells of the **upper epidermis** (leaf surface)
cells of the **lower epidermis** (except guard cells)   } do not have chloroplasts.

See also • p. 27 **Active transport** • p. 40 **Leaf structure** and **Stomata**

Transport of water and minerals – figure

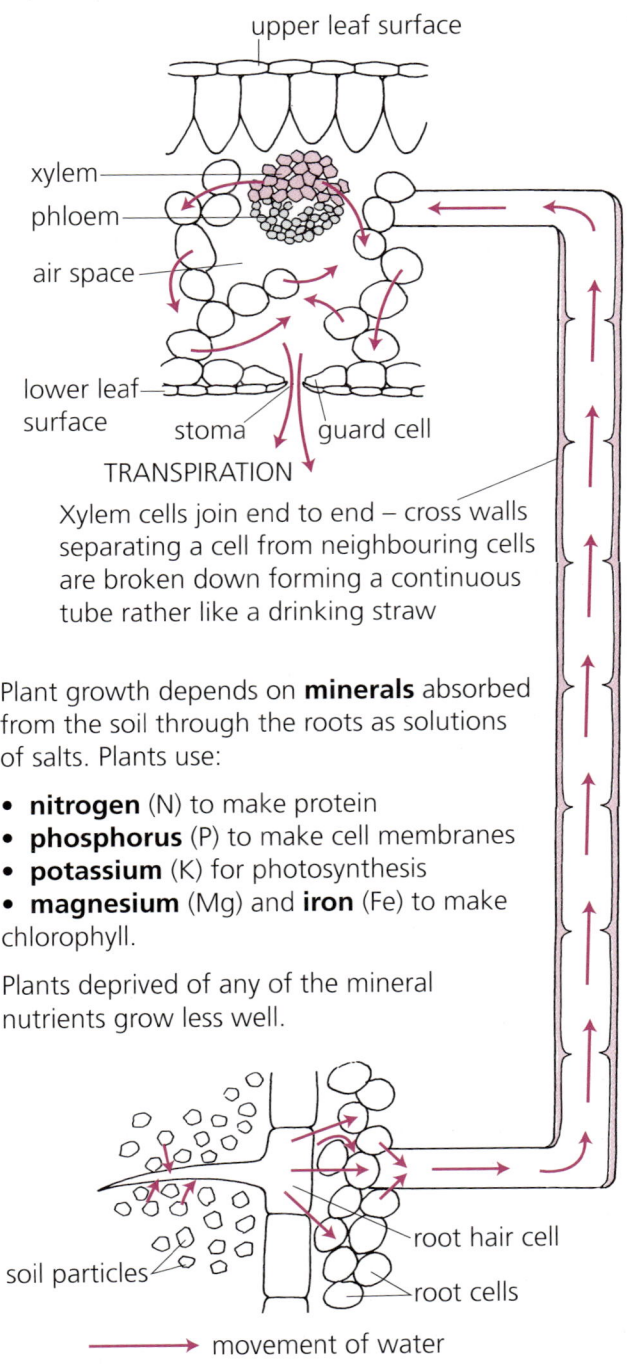

TRANSPIRATION

Xylem cells join end to end – cross walls separating a cell from neighbouring cells are broken down forming a continuous tube rather like a drinking straw

Plant growth depends on **minerals** absorbed from the soil through the roots as solutions of salts. Plants use:

- **nitrogen** (N) to make protein
- **phosphorus** (P) to make cell membranes
- **potassium** (K) for photosynthesis
- **magnesium** (Mg) and **iron** (Fe) to make chlorophyll.

Plants deprived of any of the mineral nutrients grow less well.

⟶ movement of water

Transport of food

The figure on page 45 shows the movement of food from the leaf to all parts of the plant.

- The concentration of sugar in the leaf is often lower than the concentration of sugar in the upper ends of the **sieve tubes**
  - ★ as a result sugar has to move from the leaf into the sieve tubes by **active transport**.
- Osmosis draws water from the xylem and increases the pressure in the sieve tubes
  - ★ as a result sugar solution moves to all parts of the plant through the sieve tubes – the process is called **translocation** – the **companion cells** support the function of sieve cells.
- Pressure in the sieve tubes drops as cells use sugar or store it as starch (e.g. in root cells).

The figure below shows how plants use the sugar made by photosynthesis.

sugars
- for respiration
- to make starch which is a store of food
- to make cellulose which is a component of cell walls
- to react with nitrates to form proteins

Factfile

Aphids (greenfly and blackfly) are insects which **feed** on the **sugar** transported in plants. To feed, the aphid pierces the plant with its pointed hollow **mouthparts** which are then inserted into a **sieve tube**. The **pressure** of the sugar solution in the sieve tube **forces** the liquid up the mouthparts into the insect.

Transport of food – figure

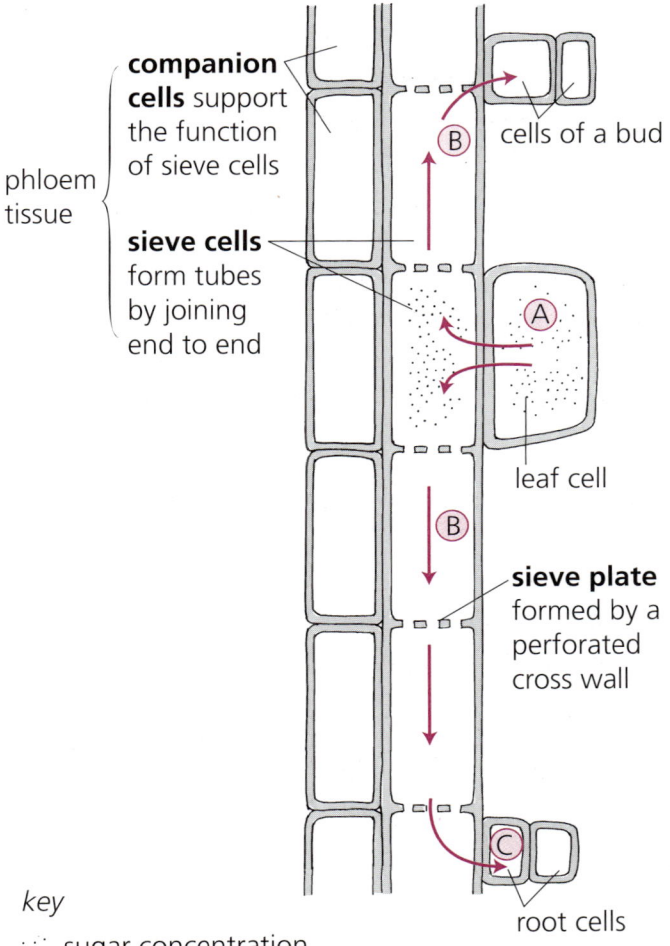

Plant responses

Plants move by growing in response to stimuli. **Nastic** movements are responses to stimuli that come from **all** directions. **Tropic** movements are responses to stimuli which come mainly from one direction (see page 47).

Tropisms are **positive** if the plant grows towards the stimulus and **negative** if it grows away. The growing tips (shoot/root) of a plant are **receptors** for different stimuli.

Auxin is an example of a plant hormone (growth substance). It is produced in the shoot tip and makes the cellulose wall of plant cells more elastic. Cells therefore elongate rapidly.

There is more auxin in the shady side of the shoot tip. The cells there grow **more** rapidly than the cells on the brightly lit side. The shoot bends towards the light and receives as much light as possible for photosynthesis.

The effect of the hormone produced by the shoot cap is different from auxin produced by the shoot tip. It **slows down** growth in the underside of the root tip and the root bends down.

Farmers and gardeners use auxin. Synthetic auxin is a **weed killer**. **Auxin paste** smeared over the carpels produces **seedless** fruit without fertilisation. The auxin in **rooting powder** encourages root growth from stem cuttings.

Factfile

- Auxin sometimes prevents growth. It diffuses down the stem and prevents the growth of side shoots. Chopping the top off a plant removes the source of auxin and side branches then develop. This is why a gardener trims a hedge to make it more bushy.

- It does **not** matter which way up a **seed** is planted. When the seed germinates, **positive phototropism** and **negative geotropism** mean that the **shoot** grows **upwards**; **positive geotropism** and **negative phototropism** mean that the **root** grows **downwards**.

Plant responses – figure

Tropisms – the response of the shoot tip to light and the root tip to gravity and water

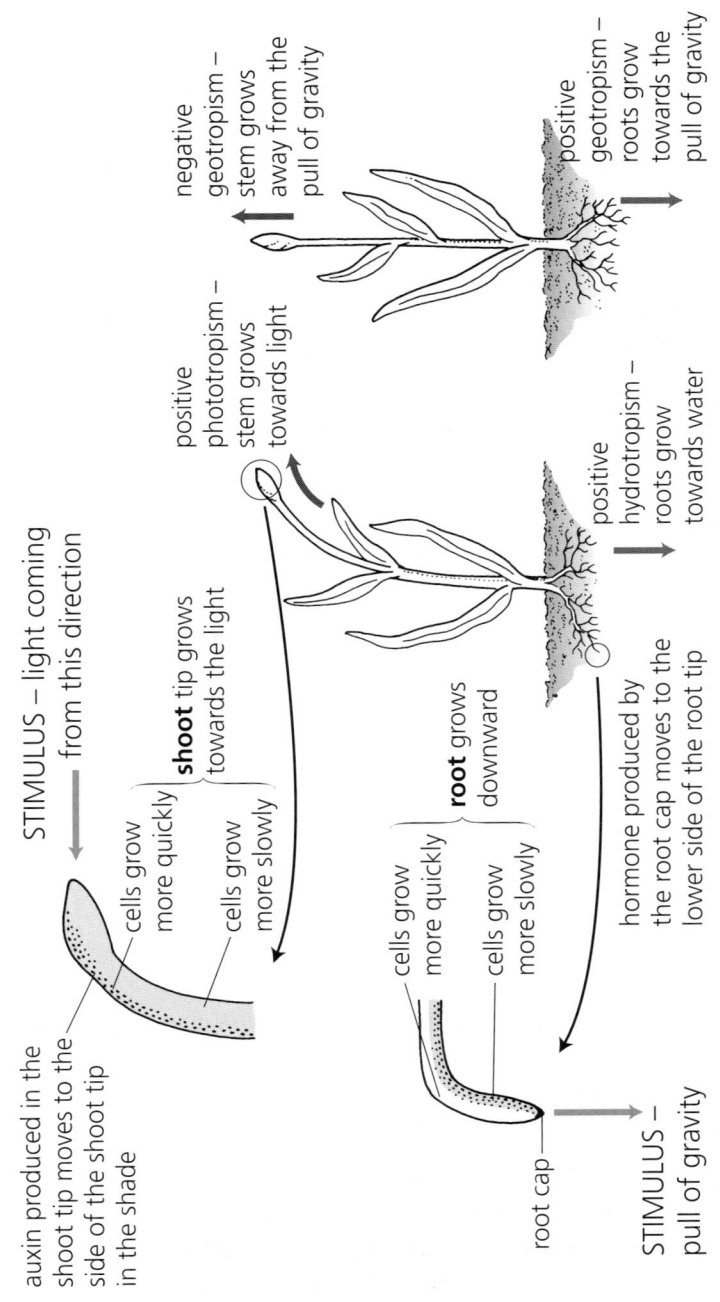

Plants as organisms quiz

Questions

1. (a) Name the inorganic substances that are the raw materials for photosynthesis.
   (b) Name the gas given off during photosynthesis.

2. Minerals are needed for healthy growth. Match each substance in column **A** with its function in column **B**.

A substances	B functions
Nitrogen	Cell membranes
Phosphorus	Chlorophyll
Magnesium	Protein

3. Compare the characteristics of xylem tissue with those of phloem tissue.

4. List the major limiting factors for photosynthesis. Briefly explain how a greenhouse overcomes the effect of limiting factors on plant growth.

5. Match items **A** with the correct descriptions **B**.

A tropisms	B descriptions
Phototropism	Water
Geotropism	Light
Hydrotropism	Gravity

Answers

1. (a) carbon dioxide and water (b) oxygen

2. | A substances | B functions |
   |---|---|
   | nitrogen | protein |
   | phosphorus | cell membranes |
   | magnesium | chlorophyll |

3. **Xylem:** dead tissue (cells): tissue (cells) waterproofed with lignin; transports water and minerals; transport of materials is one-way; xylem tissue does not have companion cells. **Phloem:** living tissue (cells): tissue (cells) not waterproofed with lignin; transport of materials is both ways; phloem tissue has companion cells.

4. temperature; light intensity; supplies of carbon dioxide; and water / a modern greenhouse provides warmth; lighting; a source of carbon dioxide; and water from sprinkler systems

5. | A tropisms | B descriptions |
   |---|---|
   | phototropism | light |
   | geotropism | gravity |
   | hydrotropism | water |

Humans as organisms: energy and transport   4

Food

Food is a source of:

- **energy** that powers life's activities
- materials for the **growth** and **repair** of the body
- substances that control the **metabolism** of cells.

The nutrients in food are **carbohydrates**, **fats**, **proteins**, **vitamins** and **minerals**. **Water** and **fibre** are also components of food. **Additives** are put into food.

The **energy value** of food is measured using an instrument called a **bomb calorimeter**. People's energy needs depend on their:

- age
- gender (male or female)
- activities.

Young people, pregnant and lactating (producing milk) women and active people need the most energy. The **metabolic rate** measures the rate at which the body uses energy. It is lowest (the **basal metabolic rate**) when the body is at rest.

A person's weight depends on the balance between the body's energy **output** (activities) and energy **input** (food intake). If output balances input then a person's weight is **constant**.

Our diet is the food and drink we take in. Choosing items from each of the basic four food groups:

- dairy food
- bread and cereals
- meat and alternatives
- fruit and vegetables

helps provide a **balanced diet**.

See also • p. 7 **Metabolism**

Food and diet – Mind Map

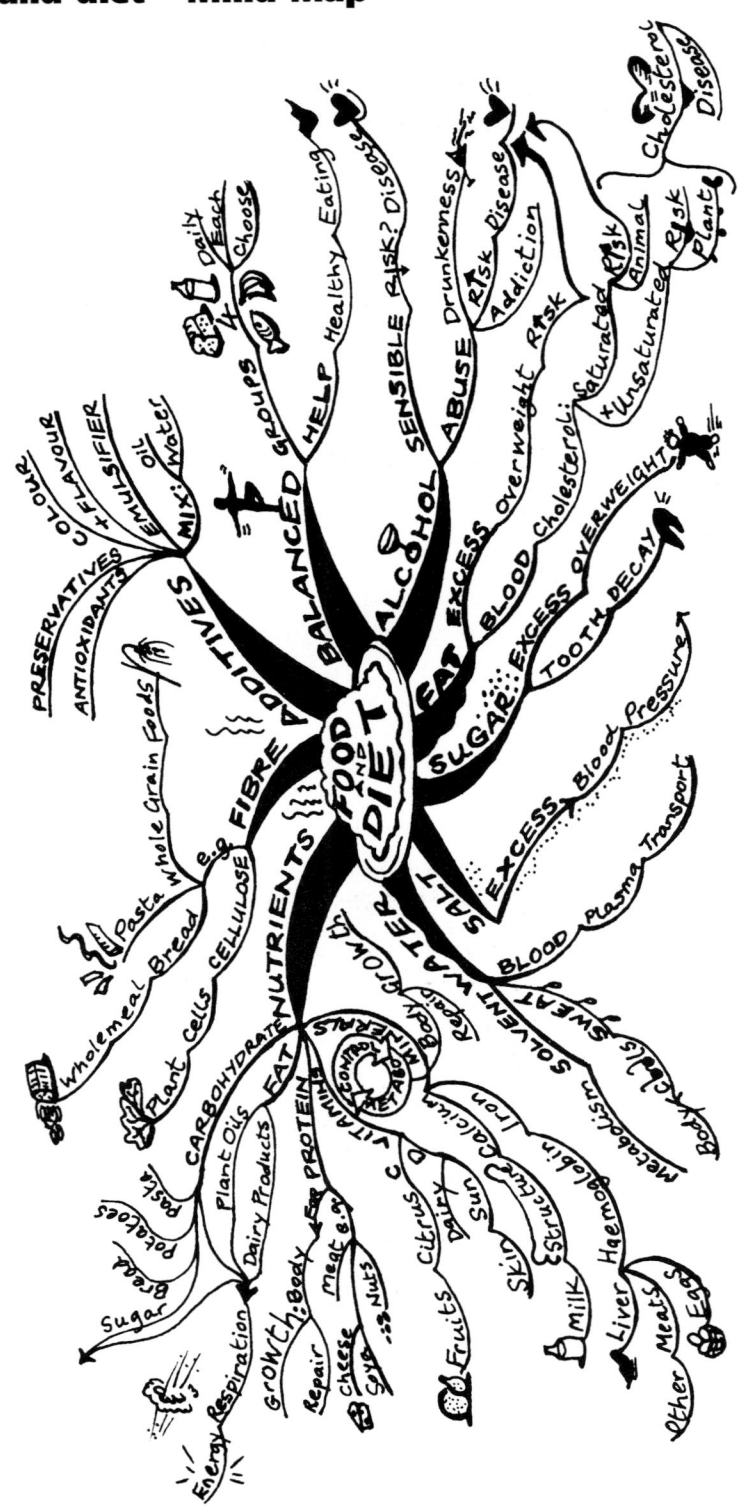

Digesting food

Food is processed through the **intestine**. The muscular action which moves food through the intestine is called **peristalsis**.

- **Ingestion** – food is taken into the mouth.
- **Digestion** – large molecules of food which the body cannot absorb are broken down into smaller molecules which the body can absorb.
- **Absorption** – the small molecules of food pass into the bloodstream.
- **Egestion** – undigested food is removed from the body through the anus.

The **liver** and **pancreas** are connected by ducts. They play an important role in the digestion of food. Digested food is **absorbed** through the wall of the **ileum** (see page 53) into the bloodstream.

The human intestine

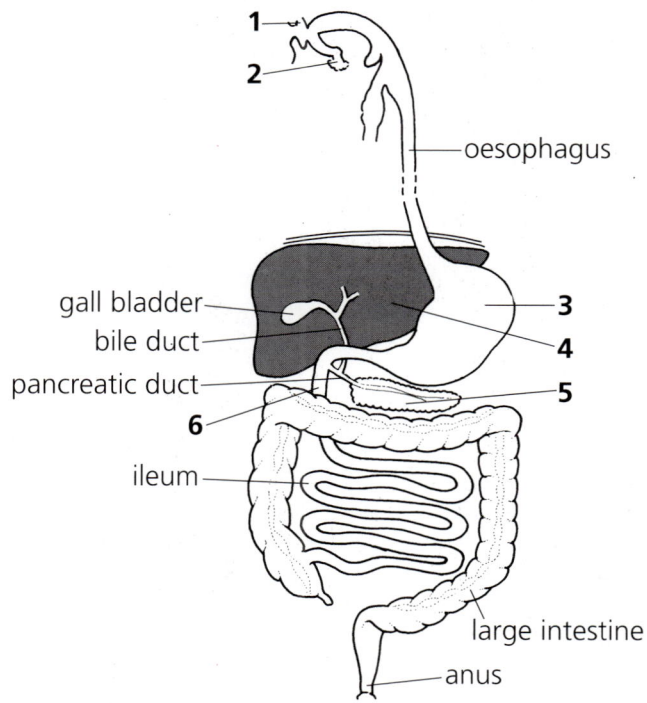

Digesting food – mouth, stomach and small intestine

(M) = mechanical processes break up the food and mix it with digestive juices.

(C) = chemical reactions digest food using different enzymes (see page 54).

The numbers on the diagram (see page 51) refer to the numbered items below.

1 (M) Teeth chew food, breaking it into small pieces. As a result:
  - ★ the surface area of food exposed to the action of digestive enzymes is increased
  - ★ food is digested more quickly.

2 (C) Saliva, produced by the salivary glands:
  - contains the enzyme amylase
  - moistens the food – making it easier to swallow.

3 (M) Muscles of the **stomach** wall and **small intestine** mix food thoroughly with different juices containing digestive enzymes.

  (C) Gastric juice, produced by **pits** in the stomach wall, contains **hydrochloric acid** and the enzymes **renin** and **pepsin**. Renin makes milk solid so that it stays a longer time in the gut and is digested. **Hydrochloric acid** increases the acidity of the stomach contents. As a result:
  - ★ bacteria in the food are killed
  - ★ the action of salivary amylase is stopped.

4 (C) Bile – produced by the **liver** – is a green alkaline liquid which is stored in the gall bladder before release into the small intestine through the bile duct.
  - Bile neutralises acid from the stomach.
  - Bile breaks fat into small droplets (**emulsification**), increasing the surface area of fat exposed to the action of the enzyme **lipase**.

5 (C) Pancreatic juice – produced by the **pancreas** – is released into the small intestine through the pancreatic duct. It contains:
  - **sodium carbonate** which neutralises stomach acid
  - **carbohydrases, proteases** and **lipases**.

6 (C) Intestinal juice – produced by glands in the wall of the **duodenum** and **ileum** contains:
  - **carbohydrases** and **lipases** that complete the digestion of carbohydrates and fats.

The ileum: absorption of digested food

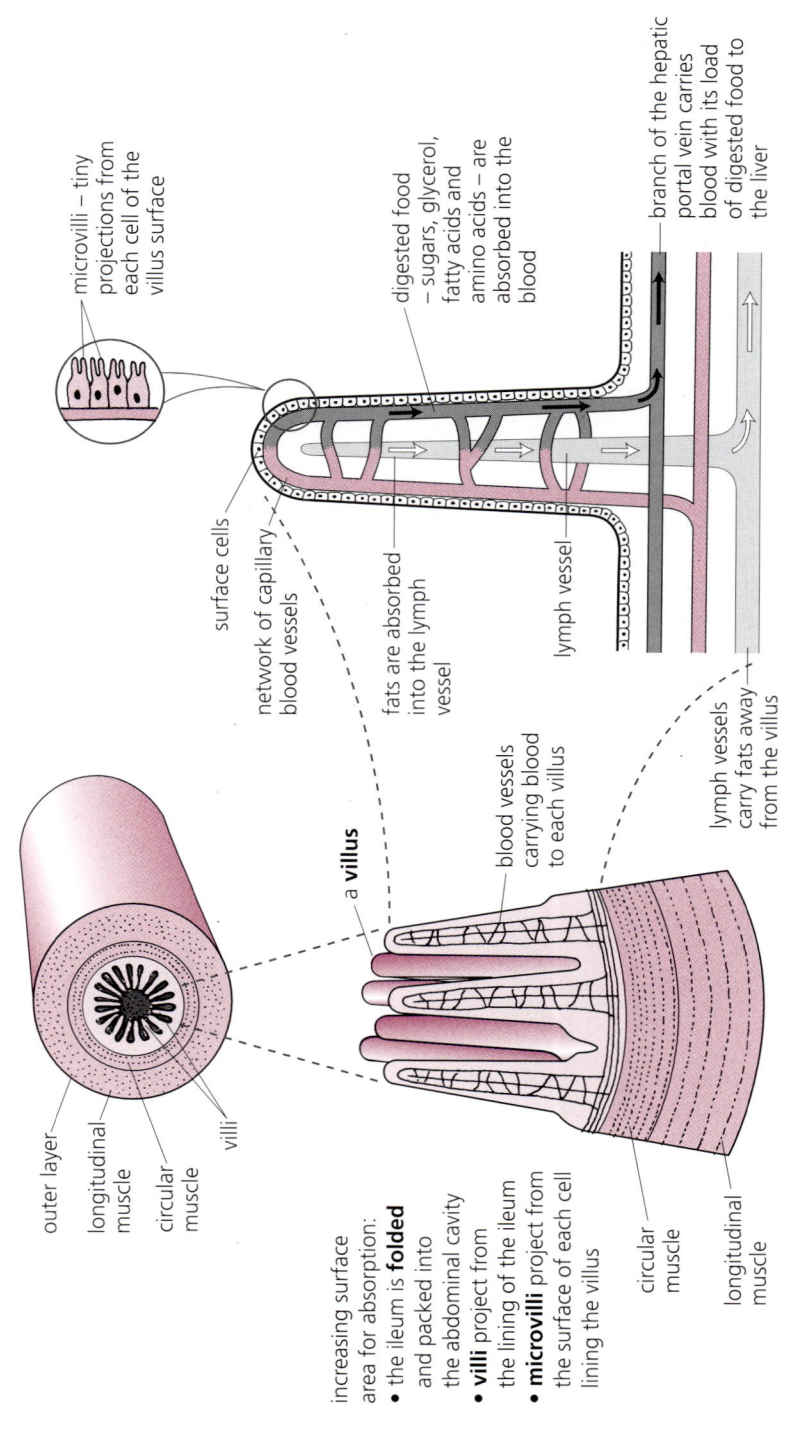

Digestive enzymes

Enzymes that digest carbohydrates, proteins and fats

Enzyme group	Example	Where found	Food component	After digestion
Carbohydrases (catalyse the digestion of carbohydrates)	Amylase	Mouth	Starch	Maltose
	Maltase	Small intestine	Maltose	Glucose
Proteases (catalyse the digestion of proteins)	Pepsin	Stomach	Protein	Polypeptides
	Chymotrypsin Dipeptidase	Small intestine	Polypeptides Dipeptides	Dipeptides Amino acids
Lipases (catalyse the digestion of fat)	Lipase	Small intestine	Fat	Fatty acids + glycerol

Quick summary

Digestive enzymes **catalyse** the breakdown of food by **hydrolysis**. Water splits large molecules of food which the body cannot absorb, into smaller molecules which can be absorbed.

Using air

Breathing air, gaseous exchange and aerobic respiration are linked processes.

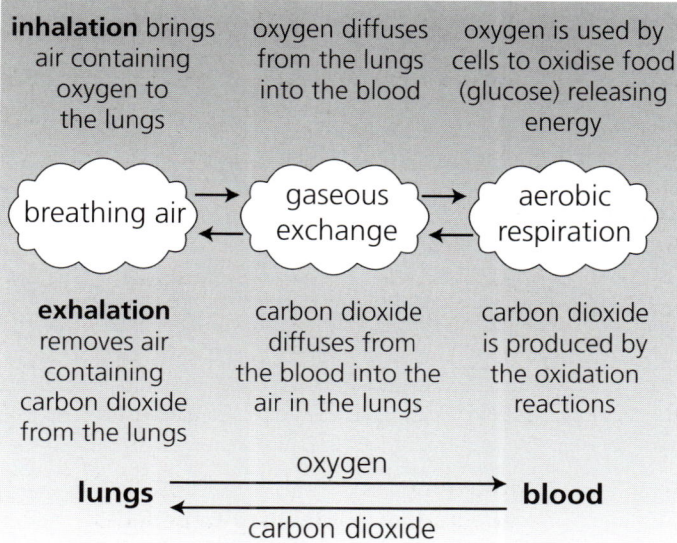

The **upper respiratory tract** is a tube from the nostrils and mouth to the lungs (see page 56). It:

- **warms** inhaled air to body temperature
- **cleans** inhaled air of dust particles and disease-causing organisms.

Note

Each **bronchus** branching from the trachea forms a network of small tubes called **bronchioles** in the lungs. The bronchioles divide into even smaller tubes which end in clusters of sac-like structures called **alveoli**.

Exam tips

Remember the distinction between **respiration** and **gaseous exchange**. **Respiration** occurs in **cells** and releases **energy** from food for life's activities. Oxygen **diffuses** from the air in the lungs into the blood, and carbon dioxide **diffuses** from the blood into the air in the lungs. The process is called **gaseous exchange**.

The lungs and upper respiratory tract

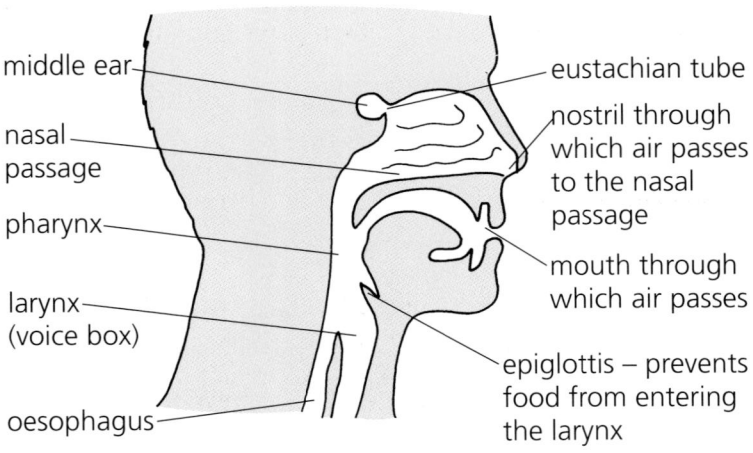

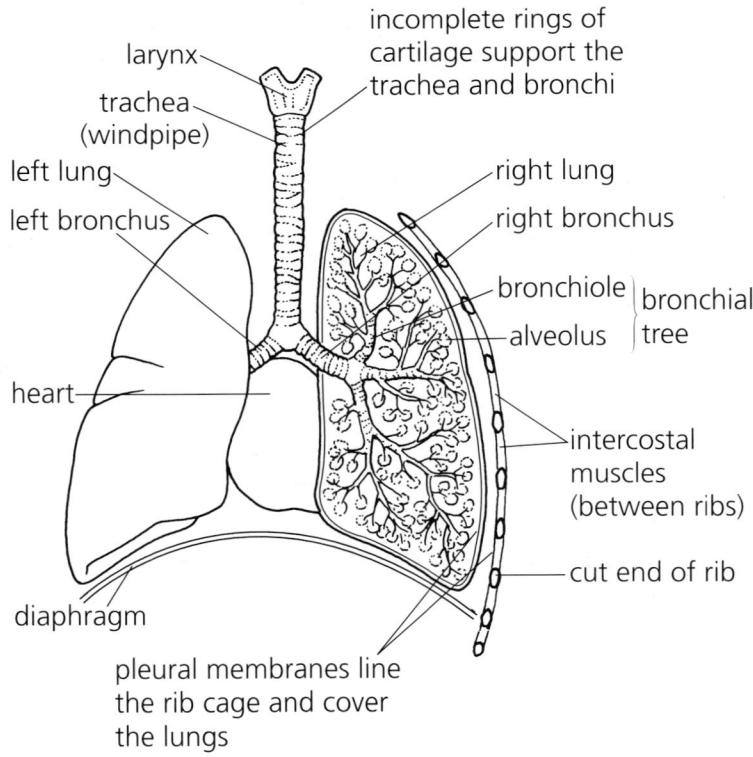

Gaseous exchange in the lungs

Exchanging gases (oxygen and carbon dioxide) takes place through the walls of the alveoli and the capillary blood vessels. The millions of alveoli in a pair of human lungs form a surface area of about 90 m². Each alveolus is adapted for the efficient diffusion of gases. It is:

- thin walled
- moist
- well supplied with blood vessels.

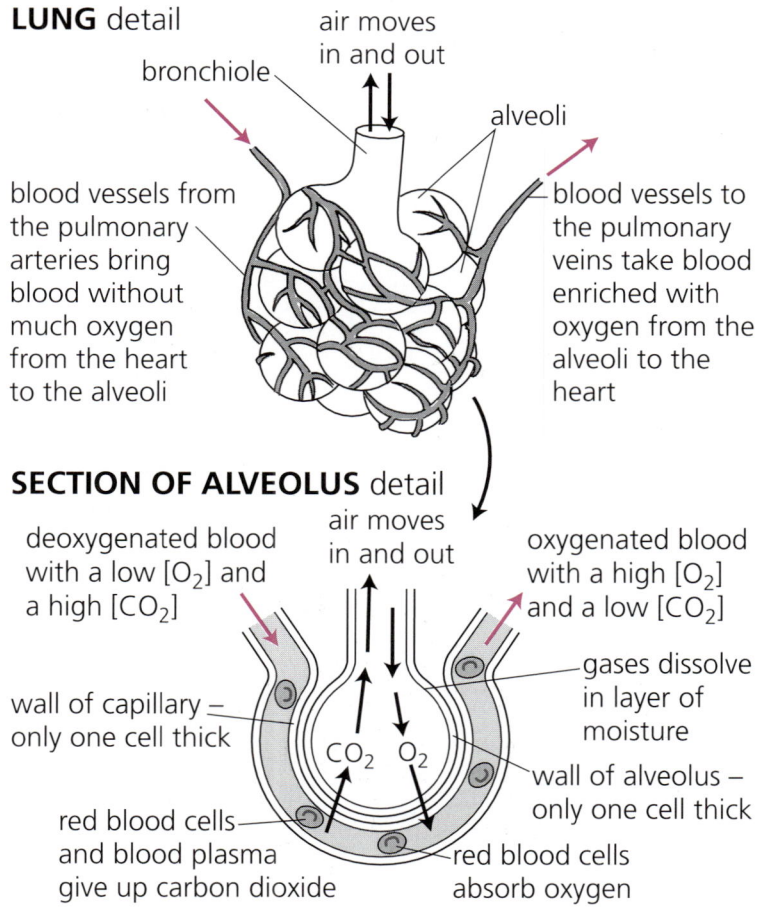

LUNG detail
- bronchiole
- air moves in and out
- alveoli
- blood vessels from the pulmonary arteries bring blood without much oxygen from the heart to the alveoli
- blood vessels to the pulmonary veins take blood enriched with oxygen from the alveoli to the heart

SECTION OF ALVEOLUS detail
- deoxygenated blood with a low [O_2] and a high [CO_2]
- air moves in and out
- oxygenated blood with a high [O_2] and a low [CO_2]
- wall of capillary – only one cell thick
- gases dissolve in layer of moisture
- red blood cells and blood plasma give up carbon dioxide
- wall of alveolus – only one cell thick
- red blood cells absorb oxygen

See also • p. 27 **Diffusion** • p. 60 **Plasma**

Breathing movements

The **ribs** and **diaphragm** form an elastic cage around the lungs. As they move, the pressure in the lungs changes. This change in pressure causes **inhaling** – breathing in – and **exhaling** – breathing out.

Inhaling and exhaling

inhaling the volume of the thoracic cavity increases – the pressure of air inside the thoracic cavity becomes less than atmospheric pressure – so air is drawn into the lungs

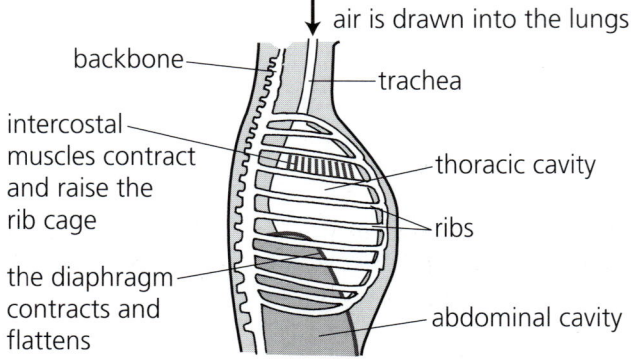

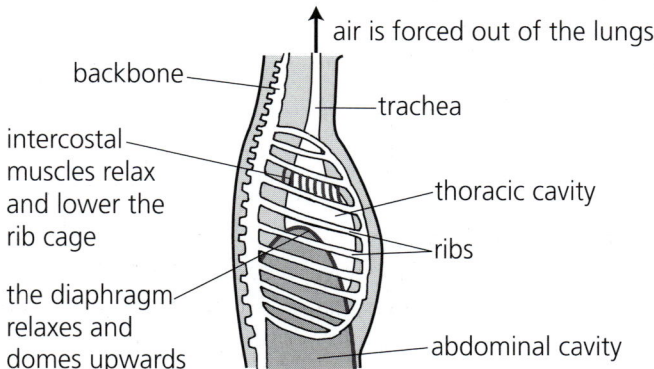

exhaling the volume of the thoracic cavity decreases – the pressure of air inside the thoracic cavity becomes greater than atmospheric pressure – so air is forced out of the lungs

Respiration

The **oxidation** of digested food substances in cells (**cellular respiration**) releases energy. The energy released powers the activities which define the characteristics of life. Cellular respiration that uses oxygen is called **aerobic respiration** and occurs in the **mitochondria** of cells.

$$\text{Glucose + Oxygen} \rightarrow \text{Carbon dioxide + Water}$$

$$C_6H_{12}O_6(aq) + 6O_2(g) \rightarrow 6CO_2(g) + 6H_2O(l)$$

Energy released = 16.1 kJ/g glucose.

Cellular respiration that does not use oxygen is called **anaerobic respiration** and occurs in the **cytoplasm** of cells.

When muscles are contracting vigorously:

$$\text{Glucose} \rightarrow \text{Lactic acid}$$

$$C_6H_{12}O_6(aq) \rightarrow 2CH_3CHOHCO_2(aq)$$

Energy released = 0.83 kJ/g glucose.

Lactic acid accumulates and an **oxygen debt** builds up. Too much lactic acid stops the muscles from working. **Panting** brings a rush of oxygen to the muscles. The lactic acid is oxidised and the oxygen debt **repaid**.

In yeast cells in the absence of oxygen:

$$\text{Glucose} \rightarrow \text{Ethanol + Carbon dioxide}$$

$$C_6H_{12}O_6(aq) \rightarrow 2C_2H_5OH(aq) + 2CO_2(g)$$

Energy released = 1.17 kJ/g glucose.

Note

The energy released during anaerobic respiration is less than in aerobic respiration. Cells do not use the energy released directly. It is converted into the energy of chemical bonds in a substance called **adenosine triphosphate** (ATP). Anaerobic respiration in yeast cells provides us with food and drink:

- ethanol is the 'alcohol' in wines and beers
- carbon dioxide puffs up bread making it rise before baking.

See also • p. 7 **Characteristics of life** • p. 26 **Mitochondria** and **Cytoplasm**
• p. 57 **Gaseous exchange**

Blood

Blood is a liquid containing different cells. The liquid is called **plasma** which consists of 90% water and 10% of materials dissolved in it:

- **blood proteins** including antibodies that defend the body against disease, enzymes and fibrinogen which helps stop bleeding
- **foods** and **vitamins**
- **hormones** which help co-ordinate different body functions.

Red blood cells are made in bone **marrow**. They have no nucleus and are packed with the pigment **haemoglobin** which gives them their red colour. Haemoglobin combines with the oxygen which diffuses from the alveoli into the bloodstream. Old red blood cells are destroyed in the liver.

White blood cells are made in the **bone marrow** and **spleen**. They do have a nucleus. There are two basic types:

- **lymphocytes** which produce **antibodies** that destroy substances/cells the body does not recognise as its own – **antigens**
- **phagocytes** that engulf substances/cells attacked by antibodies.

Platelets which look like fragments of red cells. They help to stop bleeding.

Blood cells seen under a microscope

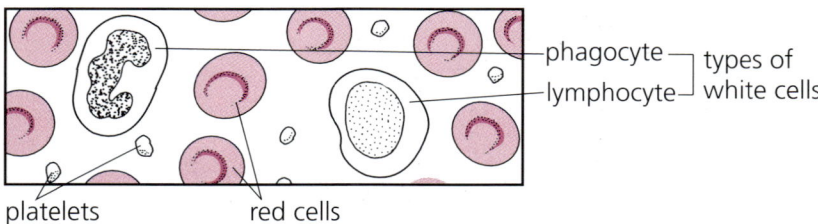

Exam tips

Remember that **red** blood cells do **not have** a **nucleus**; **white** blood cells do **have** a **nucleus**.

See also • p. 52 **Liver** • p. 57 **Aveoli** • p. 80 **Antibodies** and **Antigens**

Moving blood around

The blood system consists of tube-like vessels – **arteries**, **veins** and **capillaries** – through which blood is pumped around the body by the **heart**.

Exam hint

Make sure that you can trace the flow of blood through the heart.

Blood system

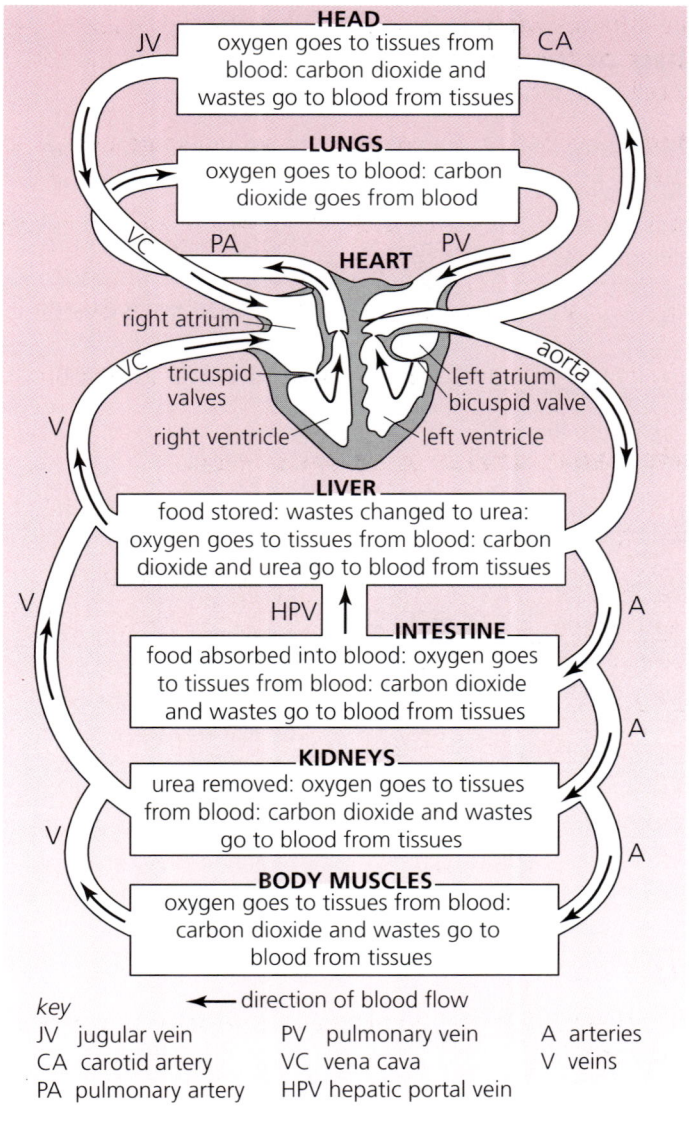

Blood vessels

- **Arteries** carry blood from the heart – the blood transports oxygen (except the pulmonary artery), digested food and other substances to the tissues and organs that need them.
- **Veins** carry blood to the heart – the blood transports carbon dioxide (except the pulmonary vein) and other wastes produced by the metabolism of cells from the tissues and organs
- **Capillaries** link arteries with veins – the exchange of materials between blood and tissues and organs occurs through the walls of the capillaries.

Comparing arteries and veins

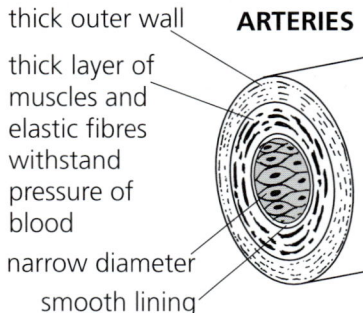

ARTERIES
- thick outer wall
- thick layer of muscles and elastic fibres withstand pressure of blood
- narrow diameter
- smooth lining

- carry blood away from the heart to organs and tissues
- blood at high pressure
- have a pulse because the vessel walls expand and relax as blood spurts from the heart

VEINS
- fairly thin outer wall
- thin layer of muscles and elastic fibres easily expand reducing resistance to the flow of blood returning to the heart
- smooth lining
- large diameter

- return blood to the heart from organs and tissues (except hepatic portal vein)
- blood at low pressure
- working body muscles squeeze the veins helping push blood to the heart
- do not have a pulse since blood flows smoothly
- have valves which ensure that blood flows in one direction only returning to the heart

Capillaries

Capillaries are tiny blood vessels, 0.001 mm in diameter. They form dense networks in the tissues of the body.

- The walls of capillary blood vessels are one cell thick
  - ★ as a result substances easily diffuse between blood in the capillaries and the surrounding tissues.
- No cell is very far away from a capillary.
- The blood in capillaries supplies nearby cells with oxygen, food and other substances – it also carries away carbon dioxide and other wastes produced by the cells' metabolism.
- **Tissue fluid** carries oxygen, food and other substances to the cells – this fluid is blood plasma that has been forced out through the thin capillary walls by the pressure of the blood inside.
- Red blood cells squeeze through the smallest capillaries in single file
  - ★ as a result the pressure drops as blood passes through the capillaries from the artery to the vein.

Capillaries at work

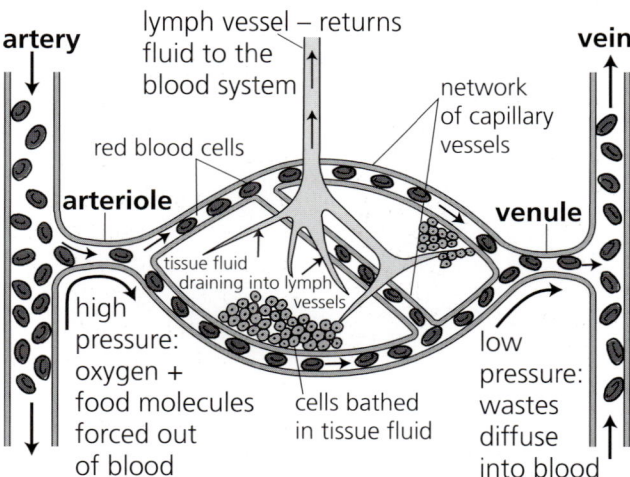

See also • p. 7 **Metabolism** • p. 60 **Plasma**

Disorders of the blood

Leukaemia is the overproduction of abnormal white blood cells.

★ As a result, red blood cell production is lowered.

Treatment is with drugs that slow the production of white blood cells and radiotherapy which kills the abnormal cells.

Haemophilia is a genetic disease. The blood does not clot properly because factor VIII – one of the substances in the blood needed for blood clots to form – is missing.

★ As a result, **haemophiliacs** (people suffering from haemophilia) lose a lot of blood if they injure themselves.

Treatment is by injection of factor VIII.

AIDS (**A**cquired **I**mmune **D**eficiency **S**yndrome) is caused by the **H**uman **I**mmunodeficiency **V**irus (**HIV**). The virus attacks a particular type of lymphocyte.

★ As a result, a person infected with HIV has reduced protection from disease-causing microorganisms.

Once HIV has destroyed a number of lymphocytes, the diseases of AIDS develop. Common diseases include:

- **pneumonia** – a disease of the lungs
- **thrush** – a fungal infection which can affect the mouth and throat
- **Kaposi's sarcoma** – a type of skin cancer.

Treatment is with drugs that **slow** the **replication** of HIV. Research worldwide is concentrating on a variety of new treatments. Development of an effective **vaccine** is one priority.

Understanding heart disease

The build-up of fatty deposits called **atheroma** in the **coronary arteries** is one cause of **heart disease**. It increases the risk of blood clots forming. A blood clot in the coronary arteries can interrupt the blood supply to the heart and the person suffers a **heart attack**. The symptoms are:

- severe pain in the chest, neck and arms
- sweating
- faintness and sickness.

The clot is called a **thrombus** and the blockage a **thrombosis**.

The risk of heart disease

BLOOD SUPPLY TO THE HEART

about 100 000 people in the UK die each year of heart disease

THE PROBLEM → UNAVOIDABLE / AVOIDABLE **RISK FACTORS**

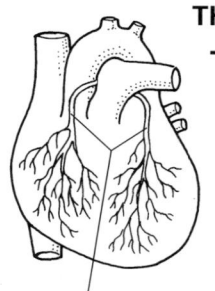

coronary arteries supply food and oxygen to the heart muscle

coronary arteries branch off the dorsal aorta

- the risk of heart disease increases with age
- men are more at risk than women
- the tendency to develop heart disease can run in families

- overweight people are more at risk
- people with high levels of cholesterol in the blood are more at risk
- permanently raised blood pressure increases the risk of heart disease and stroke
- the more stress a person suffers, the greater the risk of heart disease

Humans as organisms: energy and transport quiz

Questions

1 Match each enzyme in column **A** with its role in digestion in column **B**.

A enzymes	B roles
amylase	digests maltose to glucose
pepsin	digests fat to fatty acids and glycerol
lipase	digests starch to maltose
maltase	digests protein to polypeptides

2 Complete the following paragraph using the words below. Each word may be used once, more than once or not at all.

**thin   exhalation   fat   oxygen   inhalation   moist
carbon dioxide   exchange   alveoli   surface area**

The uptake of _____ and removal of _____ occur in the _____ of the lungs. These provide a large _____ for efficient gas _____ . They are _____-walled, have an excellent blood supply, are _____ and kept well supplied with air by breathing. _____ takes air into the lungs; _____ removes air from the lungs.

3 The different components of blood are listed in column **A**. Match each component with its correct description in column **B**.

A components	B descriptions
plasma	contain haemoglobin
red blood cells	promote the formation of blood clots
white blood cells	contains dissolved food substances
platelets	produce antibodies

Answers

1 A enzymes   B roles
amylase   digests starch to maltose
pepsin   digests protein to polypeptides
lipase   digests fat to fatty acids and glycerol
maltase   digests maltose to glucose

2 Oxygen, carbon dioxide, alveoli, surface area, exchange, thin, moist, inhalation, exhalation

3 A components   B descriptions
plasma   contains dissolved food substances
red blood cells   contain haemoglobin
white blood cells   produce antibodies
platelets   promote the formation of blood clots

Humans as organisms: coordination, control and disease   5

Coordination and the nervous system

A stimulus is a change in the environment which causes a living organism to take action. A response is the action that the organism takes. The nervous system links stimuli and responses. The process runs as follows.

stimulus	→	receptor	→	nerves	→	effector	→	response
		detects stimulus converting it into nerve impulses		transmit nerve impulses		muscles or glands which respond to nerve impulses		

Human nervous system

Neurones (nerve cells) are specialised to transmit nerve impulses. Each neurone consists of a **cell body** and **axon** which is surrounded by a sheath of fatty material called **myelin**. Bundles of neurones form **nerves** that build the nervous system.

A **reflex arc** is the chain of neurones along which nerve impulses travel to bring about a reflex (automatic) response to a stimulus. The sequence of numbered labels on the diagram on page 68 follows the process. A tiny gap called a **synapse** separates each neurone from the next neurone in the chain.

Neurotransmitter released from the end of one neurone diffuses across the synapse and stimulates the next neurone to fire off new nerve impulses.

> **Factfile**
>
> **Reflex responses** are **automatic** responses to stimuli. They happen *before* the **brain** has had time to process the information about the stimulus.

Reflex arc

Cross-section through the nerve cord

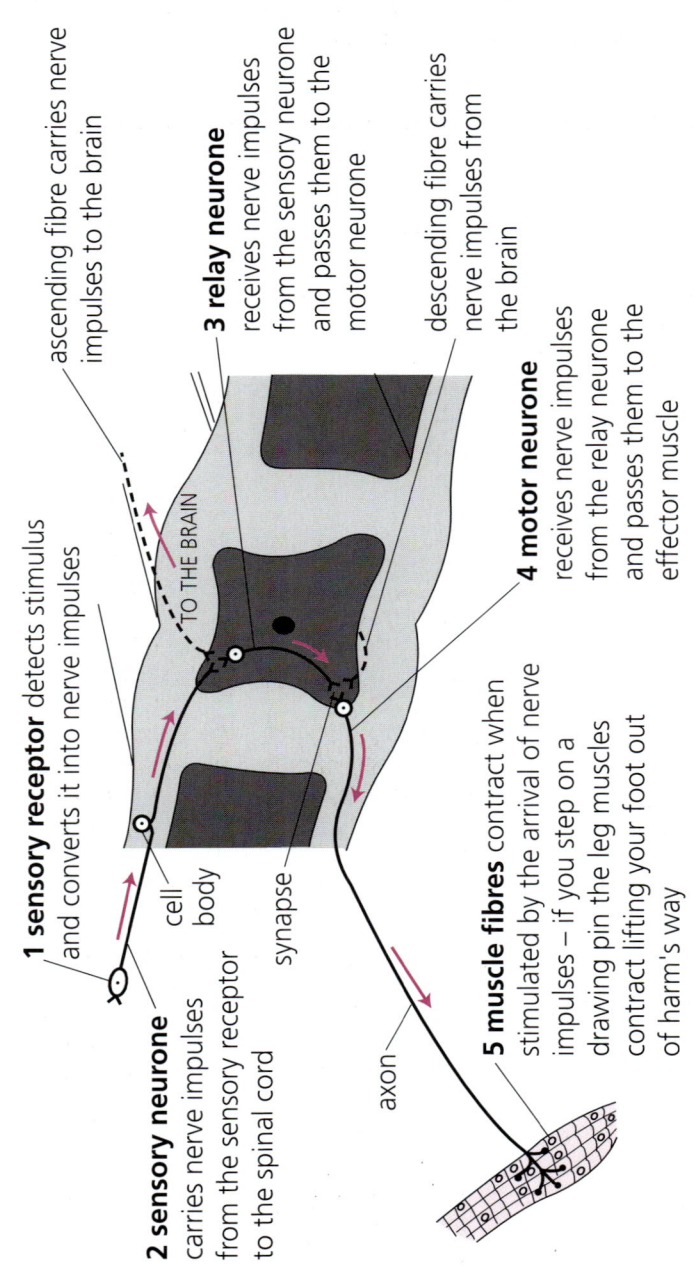

Hormones

Hormones are chemicals which regulate the activities of the body. They are produced in the tissues of the **endocrine glands** which are ductless glands that release their hormones directly into the bloodstream. The tissue on which a particular hormone(s) acts is called the **target tissue**.

Human endocrine glands and their hormones

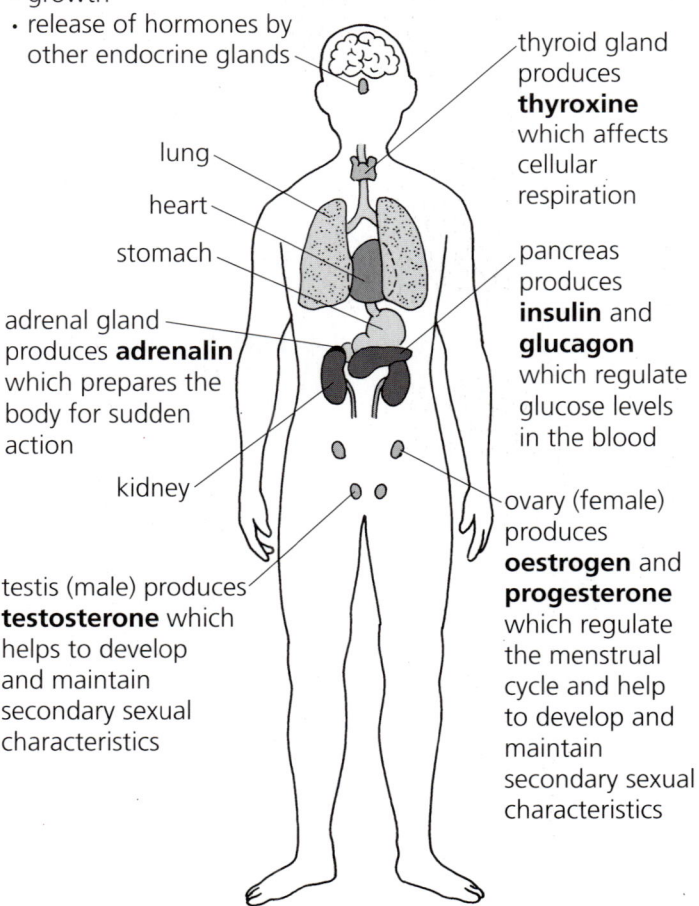

pituitary gland at base of the brain produces different hormones which affect:
- water reabsorption from the kidney tubules (ADH)
- sperm and egg production
- growth
- release of hormones by other endocrine glands

lung

heart

stomach

adrenal gland produces **adrenalin** which prepares the body for sudden action

kidney

testis (male) produces **testosterone** which helps to develop and maintain secondary sexual characteristics

thyroid gland produces **thyroxine** which affects cellular respiration

pancreas produces **insulin** and **glucagon** which regulate glucose levels in the blood

ovary (female) produces **oestrogen** and **progesterone** which regulate the menstrual cycle and help to develop and maintain secondary sexual characteristics

The menstrual cycle

The figure shows the action of the different hormones that control:

- the development and release of an egg from the human ovary
- the changes in the lining of the uterus.

The different events are the components of the **menstrual cycle** and usually occur every month during the years when a woman is fertile (approximately between ages 12–50 years).

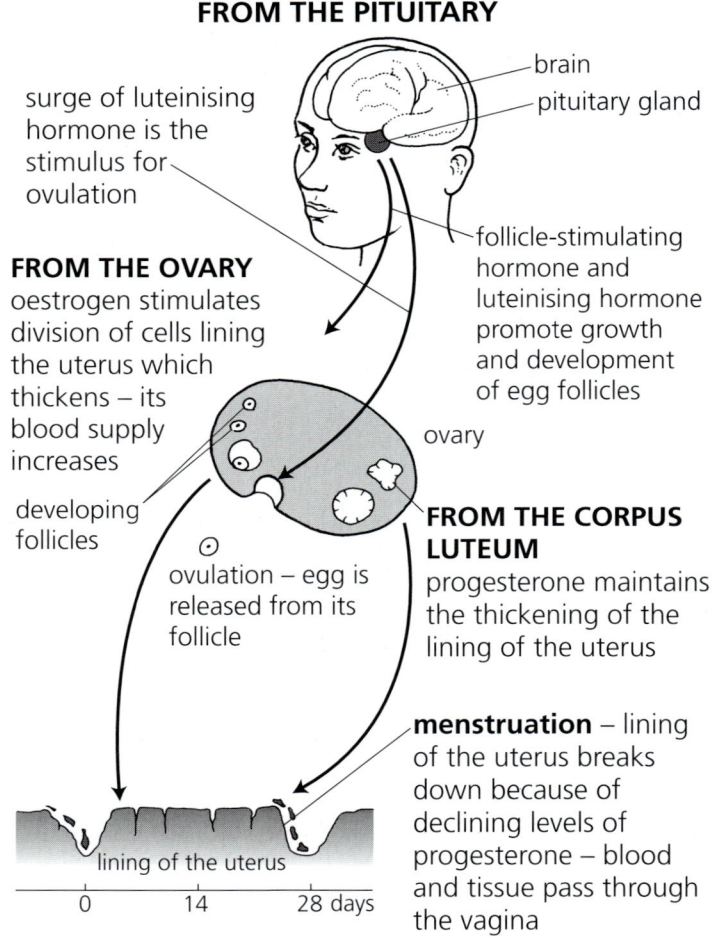

FROM THE PITUITARY

brain
pituitary gland

surge of luteinising hormone is the stimulus for ovulation

follicle-stimulating hormone and luteinising hormone promote growth and development of egg follicles

FROM THE OVARY
oestrogen stimulates division of cells lining the uterus which thickens – its blood supply increases

ovary

developing follicles

ovulation – egg is released from its follicle

FROM THE CORPUS LUTEUM
progesterone maintains the thickening of the lining of the uterus

menstruation – lining of the uterus breaks down because of declining levels of progesterone – blood and tissue pass through the vagina

lining of the uterus
0   14   28 days

Regulating glucose

The hormones **insulin** and **glucagon** help regulate the level of glucose (sugar) in the blood.

- High concentrations of blood glucose promote the release of insulin.
- Low concentrations of blood glucose promote the release of glucagon.
  - ★ As a result the concentration of glucose is regulated at around 90 mg of glucose per 100 cm³ of blood.

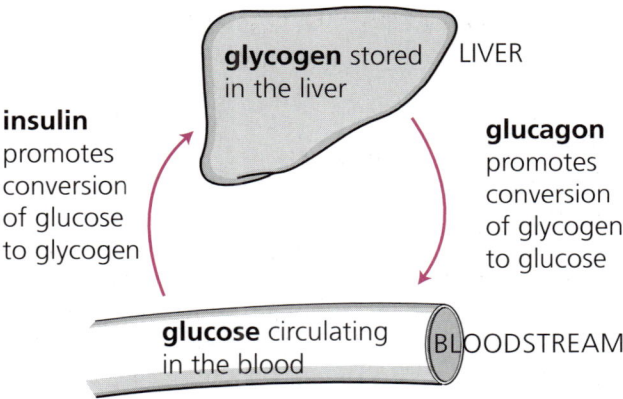

Flight or fight

The hormone **adrenalin** is released in response to sudden shock. It prepares the body for sudden action:

- cells metabolise glucose faster
  - ★ as a result more energy is available for sudden action
- the heart beats more rapidly
  - ★ as a result more blood with its load of glucose reaches tissues and organs more rapidly
- blood is diverted to tissues such as the muscles and brain.

> ### Factfile
> Most **hormones** produce their effects rather **slowly**. They bring about **long-term** changes in the body such as growth and sexual development. The hormone **adrenalin** is an **exception** to the rule.

See also • p. 7 **Metabolism** • p. 33 **Glycogen**

Homeostasis

Keeping conditions in the body constant is called **homeostasis**.

The kidneys at work

Each kidney (see page 73) consists of about one million tiny tubules called nephrons. Each nephron (see page 74) is the structure that brings about homeostatic control of the:

- concentration of salts in the body
- water content of the body.

The nephron also excretes **urea** and other wastes from the body. The sequence of numbered labels on the diagram on page 74 follows the process.

Controlling the body's water content

- **Sensory receptors** in the brain detect how much water is in the blood.
- The **pituitary gland** at the base of the brain produces **anti-diuretic hormone** (ADH) which affects the permeability of the walls of the collecting duct of the nephron.

Lots of water in the body:

- Production of ADH from the pituitary gland is reduced
  - ★ as a result most of the surplus water is excreted through the kidneys.

Less water in the body:

- Production of ADH from the pituitary gland is increased
  - ★ as a result the walls of the collecting duct of the nephron are more permeable ('leaky') to water and water is absorbed back into the body.

Where does urea come from?

- **Amino acids** in excess of the body's needs are broken down in the liver.
- The process is called **deamination**.
- **Urea** is formed and excreted in the **urine**.

Quick summary

Homeostasis depends on **negative feedback** mechanisms which enable different processes to correct themselves when they change. In other words the processes of life are **self-adjusting**.

See also • p. 34 **Amino acids** and **proteins** • p. 69 **Hormones**

Kidneys

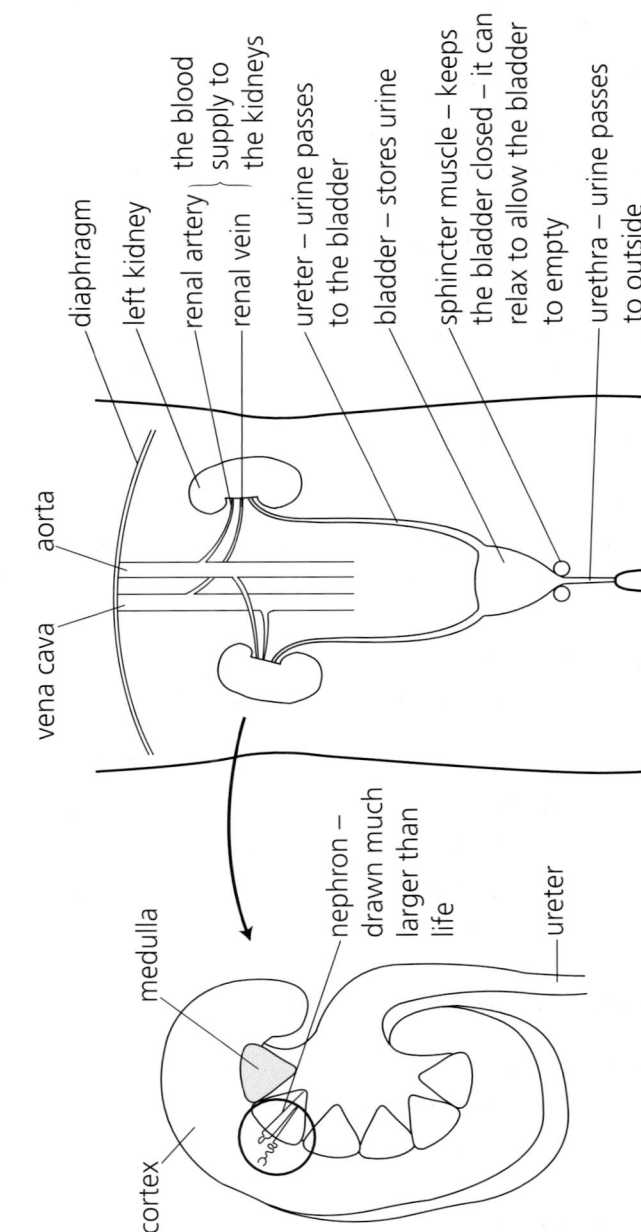

The working nephron

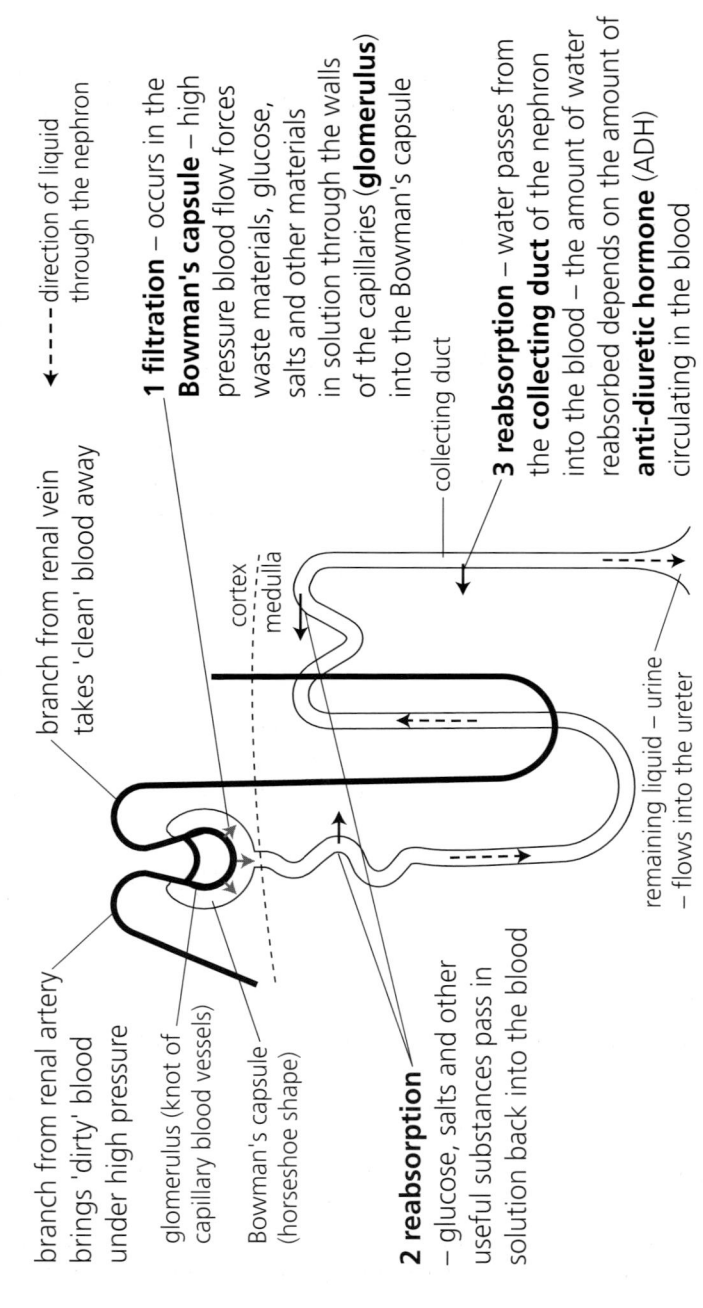

The skin and control of body temperature

The skin regulates the body's temperature.

- **Hairs** raised by erector muscles trap a layer of air which insulates the body in cold weather (air is a poor conductor of heat); in warm weather the hair is lowered and no air is trapped.
- **Fat** insulates the body and reduces heat loss.
- **Sweat** cools the body because it carries heat energy away from the body as it evaporates.
- Millions of temperature-sensitive sense receptors cover the skin; nerves connect receptor stimuli to the brain – the brain controls the body's response to changes in environmental temperature.
- When it is warm, blood vessels in the skin dilate – **vasodilation** – more blood flows through the vessels in the skin therefore heat is lost to the environment; in cold weather the blood vessels in the skin constrict – **vasoconstriction** – and less heat is lost to the environment.

Factfile

At **41°C**, the mean **core body temperature** of birds is more than that of mammals at a mean of **37°C**. The energy needed for flying comes from a **high rate** of **metabolism** which accounts for the high mean core body temperature of birds.

Quick quiz

Why are animals called either warm-blooded or cold-blooded?

Answer

Warm-blooded animals (**birds** and **mammals**) are able to keep the temperature at the centre of the body (**core** temperature) **constant** even when the temperature of the environment in which they live **changes**. The core body temperature of cold-blooded animals (**invertebrates, fish, amphibia** and **reptiles**) **changes** with changes in the temperature of the environment.

See also • p. 7 **Metabolism** • p. 68 **Receptors**

Section through the skin

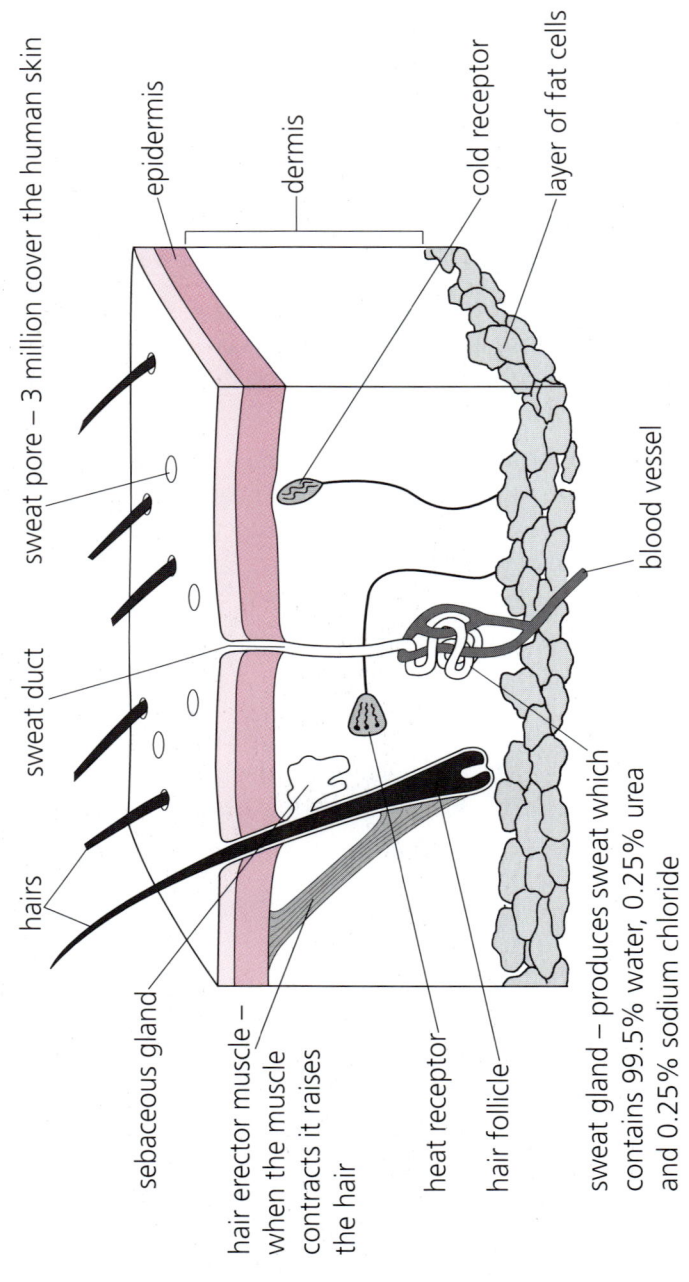

Reproduction – Mind Map

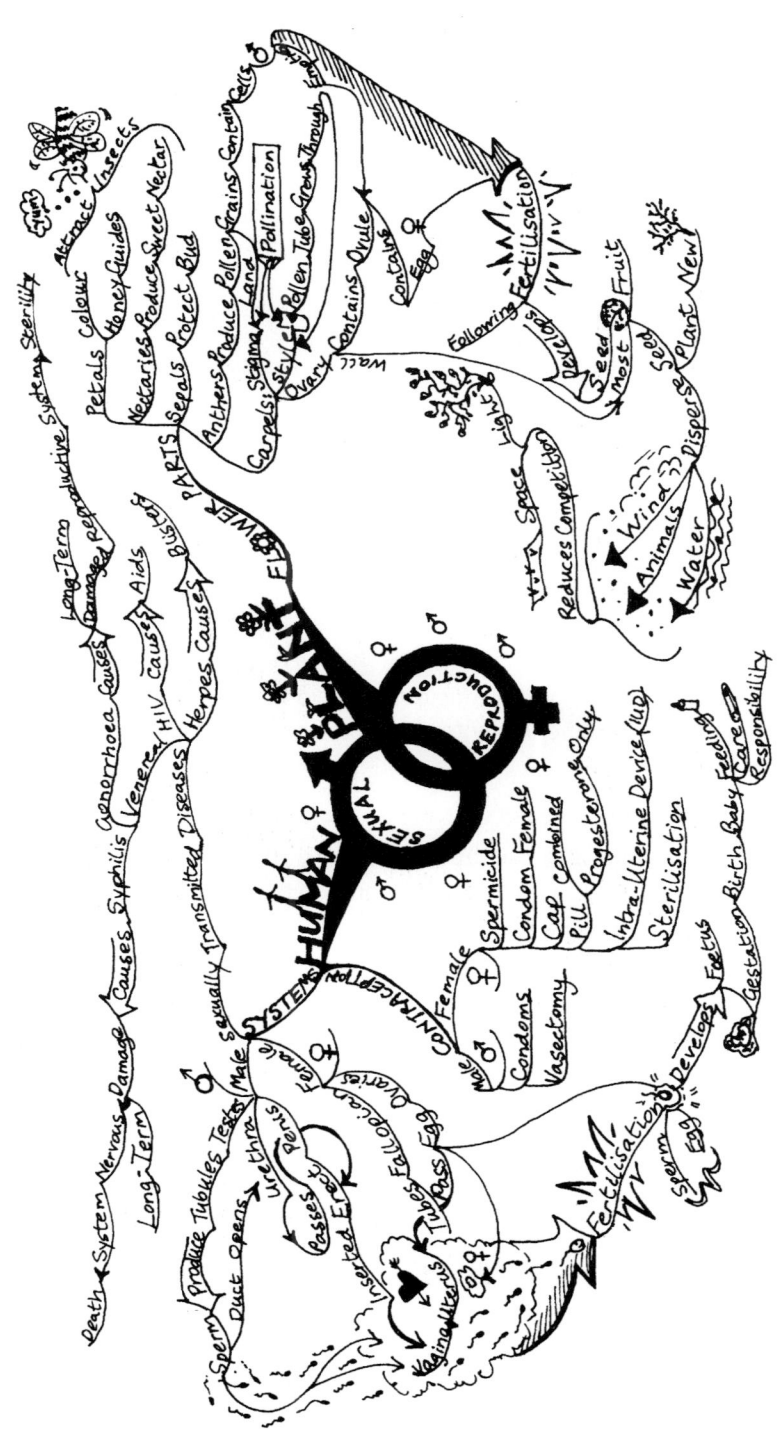

What is disease?

Infectious diseases are caused by a range of organisms which pass from person to person:

- **bacteria**, e.g. cholera, typhoid fever, tuberculosis
- **viruses**, e.g. AIDS, 'flu, German measles
- **fungi**, e.g. thrush, athlete's foot, ringworm
- **protists**, e.g. malaria, sleeping sickness.

Non-infectious diseases develop because the body is not working properly:

- **cancer** – uncontrolled cell division leads to the development of a cancerous growth (tumour)
- **degenerative illnesses** – organs and tissues work less well with wear and tear, e.g. joints become arthritic
- **allergies** – reactions to substances which are normally harmless, e.g. hayfever
- **deficiency** – inadequate intake of vitamins and other essential substances, e.g. scurvy (deficiency of vitamin C).

Genetic diseases result from genetic defects and may be inherited. Genetic make-up also influences our vulnerability to other diseases such as diabetes and heart disease.

- **Down's syndrome** is caused by an extra copy of chromosome 21.
- **Sickle-cell anaemia** is caused by a mutation of the gene – **allele** – controlling the synthesis of the blood pigment haemoglobin.
- **Haemophilia** is caused by the mutation of an allele on the X chromosome.

Factfile

Organisms that **cause** disease are called **pathogens**. **Bacteria** are a major cause of disease in **animals**. In plants, bacteria are less of a hazard but **fungi** causing disease are a major **problem**.

See also • p. 9 **Bacteria, fungi, protists** • p. 49 **Vitamins** • p. 86 **Alleles** • p. 92 **Mutation**

Lifestyles and disease

Cigarette smoke contains various substances harmful to health.

- **Nicotine** increases the heart rate and blood pressure.
- **Carbon monoxide** combines 300 times more readily with haemoglobin than oxygen does
    - ★ as a result, the level of oxygen in the blood is reduced.
- Tar contains many compounds which cause cancer (**carcinogens**).

Smoking cigarettes is a major cause of **lung cancer** and **heart disease**. Some substances in cigarette smoke irritate the membrane lining the upper respiratory tract.

- Extra mucus (phlegm) forms in the trachea and bronchi
    - ★ as a result 'smokers cough' may destroy the walls of the alveoli causing **emphysema** – the affected person easily becomes breathless.
- Particles and microorganisms enter the lungs increasing the risk of infection.

Other substances in cigarette smoke stop the **cilia** lining the upper respiratory tract from beating.

Some **drugs** are highly **addictive** and may be **abused** (e.g. cocaine, heroin). This means they are used for non-medical purposes.

Alcohol (ethanol in beers, wine and spirits) depresses the activity of the nervous system. It affects areas of the brain which control judgement.

Solvents in glues, paints, nail varnish and cleaning fluids (dry cleaners) readily produce a vapour at room temperature. Breathing them in gives a warm sense of well-being but also produces dangerous disorientation.

Factfile

Many non-infectious diseases can be avoided, or their onset delayed providing we live sensibly. **SMOKING AND 'DOING DRUGS'** are **not** healthy lifestyles.

See also • p. 55 **Upper respiratory tract**

Fighting disease

The body's natural defences against disease are:

mucus – lines the upper respiratory tract – traps bacteria and particles and is swept away by cilia

stomach – glands produce hydrochloric acid which kills bacteria on food

cervix – (part of the female reproductive system) – is plugged with mucus which is a barrier to microorganisms

tears – contain the enzyme lysozyme which destroys bacteria

skin – glands produce an oily substance called sebum which kills bacteria and fungi

white blood cells – are produced in the bone marrow and lymph glands – they destroy bacteria and other organisms which cause disease

White blood cells

Two types of white blood cell, **lymphocytes** and **phagocytes**, protect the body. They destroy bacteria, viruses or other cells or substances which may cause disease and which the body does not recognise as its own. Such materials 'foreign' to the body are called **antigens**.

- **B-lymphocytes** produce **antibodies** which are proteins that attack antigens – antibodies produced against a particular antigen will attack only that antigen; the antibody is said to be **specific** to that antigen.

- **T-lymphocytes** are also specific in their action – they do not produce antigens but instead bind with an antigen and destroy it.

Phagocytes engulf and destroy antigens (see page 81). Some phagocytes pass through tissue to attack antigens that have entered the body through cuts or scratches causing an **inflammatory response**.

B-lymphocytes produce antibodies; phagocytes engulf bacteria

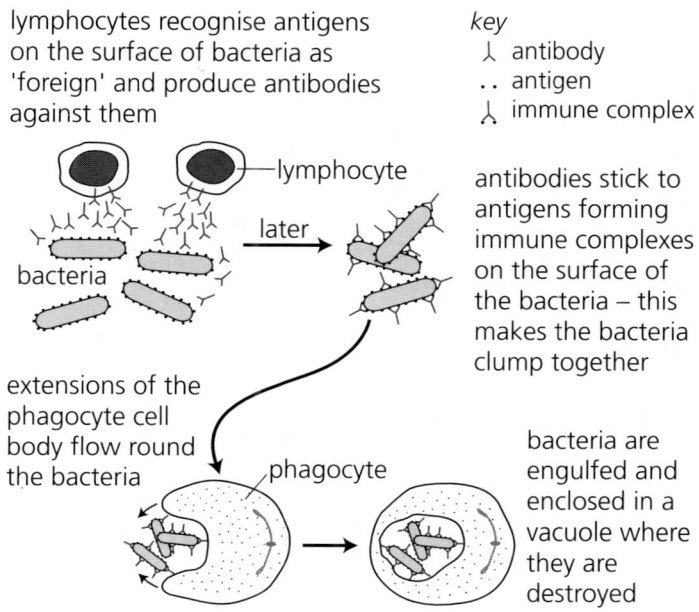

Drugs

Drugs are used to help in the fight against disease. For example:

- **Antibiotics** are used to attack the different types of bacteria that cause disease.
- **Analgesics** are drugs that reduce pain (painkillers).

Hygiene

- **Disinfectants** are chemicals that kill microorganisms – they are used to keep surfaces (e.g. in the kitchen and bathroom) clean and free from microorganisms.
- **Antiseptics** are usually weaker than disinfectants – they are used to clean wounds or an area of the skin before hypodermic injection.
- **Aseptic** procedures aim to prevent microorganisms from infecting wounds. In surgery:
  - sterilised gowns, gloves and face masks are worn by everyone in the operating theatre
  - air entering the operating theatre is filtered
  - all surfaces and equipment are easy to clean.

Humans as organisms: coordination, control and disease quiz

Questions

1 Match each body structure in column **A** with its role in the defence of the body against disease in column **B**.

A body structure	B roles
tear gland	produces sebum which kills bacteria and fungi
glands in the stomach wall	white cells produce antibodies which destroy antigens
skin	produce hydrochloric acid which kills bacteria
cilia lining the upper respiratory tract	produces the enzyme lysozyme which destroys bacteria
blood	sweep away mucus containing trapped microorganisms and particles

2 Briefly explain (a) why raised body hair helps us keep warm (b) why sweating helps us keep cool.

3 The components of the reflex arc are listed as follows: **sensory neurone, effector, relay neurone, receptor, motor neurone**.
Write the components in their correct order.

4 The structures of the kidney tubule and its blood supply are listed below. Rewrite them in the order in which a molecule of urea passes from the renal artery to the outside of the body: **tubule, urethra, bladder, glomerulus, Bowman's capsule, ureter, collecting duct**.

5 What are hormones and how are they transported around the body?

Answers

1 **A body structures** — **B roles**
tear gland — produces the enzyme lysozyme which destroys bacteria
glands in the stomach wall — produce hydrochloric acid which kills bacteria
skin — produces sebum which kills bacteria and fungi
cilia lining the upper respiratory tract — sweep away mucus containing trapped microorganisms and particles
blood — white cells produce antibodies which destroy antigens

2 (a) raised hairs trap a layer of air which insulates the body in cold weather / air is a poor conductor of heat (b) sweat cools the body because it carries heat energy away from the body as it evaporates

3 receptor, sensory neurone, relay neurone, motor neurone, effector

4 glomerulus, Bowman's capsule, tubule, collecting duct, ureter, bladder, urethra

5 hormones are chemical substances which circulate in the blood

Inheritance and evolution   6

Reproduction

There are two types of reproduction. Each type passes genetic material on from parent(s) to offspring.

Sexual reproduction in humans

Two parents (male and female) each produce **sex cells**. The male produces **sperm**; the female produces **eggs**. Sperm and eggs are formed by **meiosis**. During **fertilisation** sperm and egg fuse, forming a zygote. The **zygote** divides repeatedly by **mitosis**, producing a ball of cells called an **embryo** which develops into the new individual. The figure below shows the process in humans.

Development of the zygote

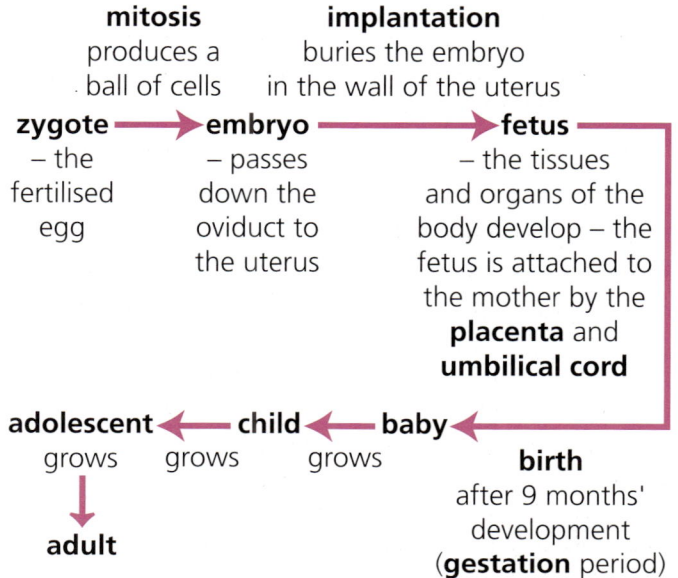

See also • p. 30 **Daughter cells** • p. 31 **Meiosis and Mitosis** • p. 92 **Variation**   83

Sexual reproduction in flowering plants

In flowering plants sexual reproduction involves **pollination**, **fertilisation** and the formation of **fruits** and **seeds**. The figure below shows the sequence.

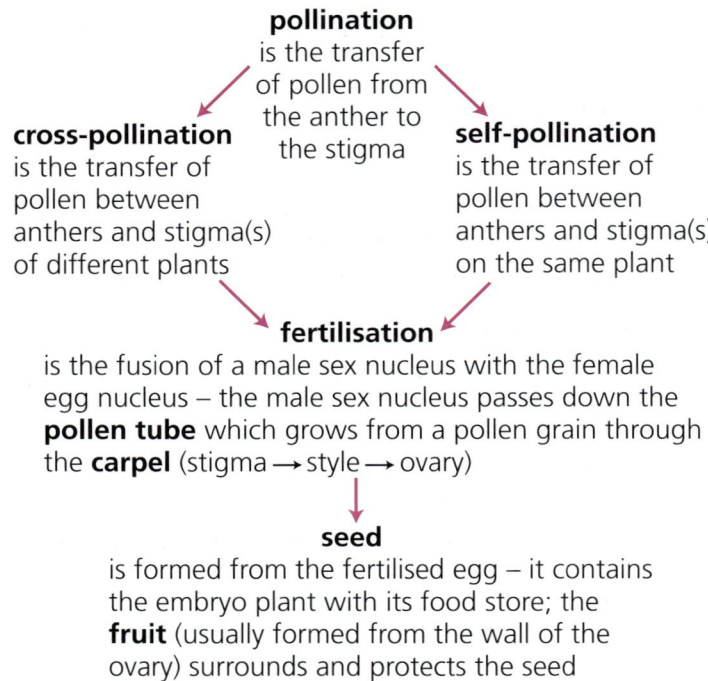

The offspring formed by sexual reproduction inherit genes from each parent. They are therefore genetically **different** from one another and their parents. The genetic differences are an important source of **variation**.

Quick quiz

Briefly explain **two** different ways in which **pollination** occurs in plants.

Answer

Insects are attracted to flowers and pick up a load of pollen and transfer it to another flower. **Wind** blows pollen from flower to flower.

Flowers are adapted for pollination:

- insect-pollinated flowers are brightly coloured and produce nectar and scent to attract insect visitors
- wind-pollinated flowers are often a dull colour and are adapted to distribute large quantities of pollen far and wide.

Fruits and seeds are adapted for distribution by either animals or wind.

Asexual reproduction

The cells of one parent divide by mitosis to produce daughter cells which form new individuals. These offspring are genetically **identical** to one another and to their parent. Variation between individuals is therefore limited to genetic changes which are the result of **mutation**. Methods of asexual reproduction are:

- **fission** – the parent cell divides into equal parts
- **budding** – outgrowths (buds) of the parent's body separate from the parent – each one becomes a separate individual
- **vegetative parts** of the parent body grow into new individuals, e.g. stems sprout roots and grow into new plants
- **regeneration** – pieces of the parent body grow into new individuals
- **parthenogenesis** – the unfertilised egg develops into a new individual.

Factfile

For gardeners, glasshouse owners and farmers, the advantages of asexual methods are that offspring are the same giving consistent quality, and that the desirable characteristics of the parent are retained from one generation to the next.

Quick summary

Different parts of a **single** plant can reproduce **asexually** into new individuals. The parts, called **vegetative** parts, are formed from the **root**, **leaf** or **stem**. The new individuals are **identical** to each other and the parent. They form a **clone**.

Monohybrid inheritance

The study of how offspring inherit characteristics from their parents is called **genetics**:

- the inheritance of a **single** characteristic is called **monohybrid inheritance**
- paired genes controlling a particular characteristic are called **alleles**
- if the alleles of a pair controlling a characteristic are identical, then the individual is **homozygous** for that characteristic
- if the alleles of a pair controlling a characteristic are different then the individual is **heterozygous** for that characteristic
- an allele which is **expressed** (produces the characteristic it controls) in preference to the form of the characteristic controlled by the allele's partner is said to be **dominant**; the partner allele is said to be **recessive** and is expressed only in the absence of its dominant partner
- all of the genes of an individual make up its **genotype**
- the characteristics produced as a result of those genes actively expressing themselves form the individual's **phenotype** (e.g. appearance).

The figure on page 87 shows how the height of pea plants is inherited.

Note

- letters are used to symbolise alleles
- a capital letter is used to symbolise the dominant member of a pair of alleles (**T** = tall)
- a small letter is used to symbolise the recessive member of a pair of alleles (**t** = short)
- the letter used to symbolise the recessive allele is the same letter as that for the dominant allele.

People behind the science

Gregor Mendel was a monk who lived in the Augustinian monastery at the town of Brunn (now Brno in the Czech Republic). He observed the **inheritance** of different characteristics in **pea plants.** His work established the basis of modern **genetics**.

How alleles controlling a characteristic (height) pass from one generation to the next

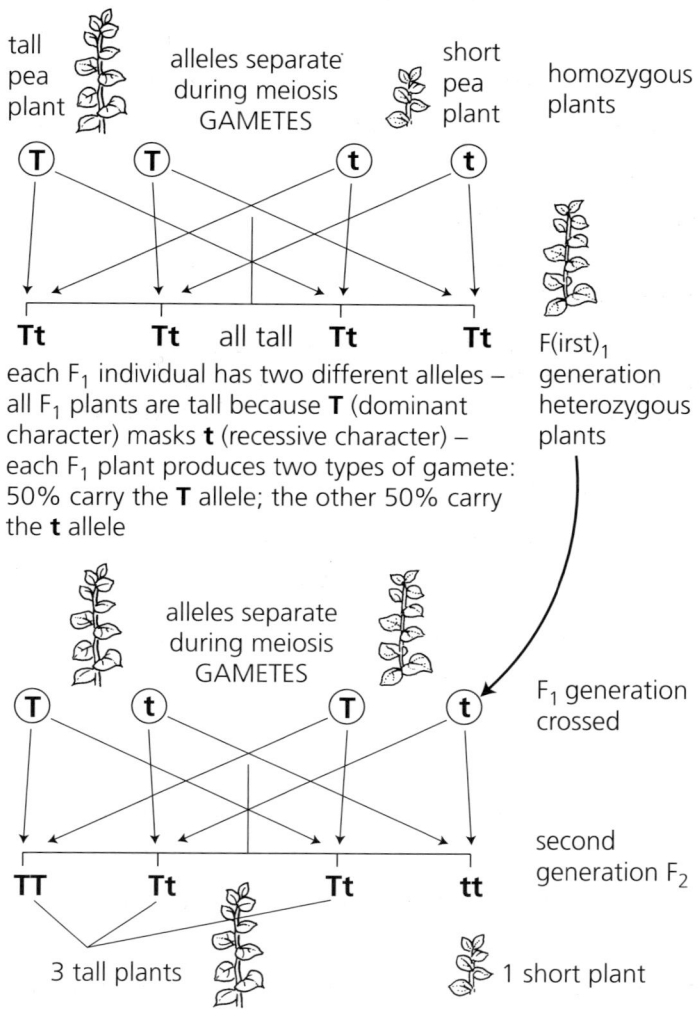

tall pea plant — alleles separate during meiosis GAMETES — short pea plant — homozygous plants

Tt   Tt   all tall   Tt   Tt   F(irst)₁ generation heterozygous plants

each F₁ individual has two different alleles — all F₁ plants are tall because **T** (dominant character) masks **t** (recessive character) — each F₁ plant produces two types of gamete: 50% carry the **T** allele; the other 50% carry the **t** allele

alleles separate during meiosis GAMETES

F₁ generation crossed

TT   Tt   Tt   tt   second generation F₂

3 tall plants   1 short plant

not all the tall plants have the same combination of alleles: 50% are heterozygous — they have both dominant and recessive alleles (**Tt**), 25% of plants are homozygous tall (**TT**); the remaining 25% are homozygous short (**tt**)

See also • p. 30 **Meiosis**

Inheritance of sex

X and **Y** chromosomes determine the sex of a person. The larger chromosome is the X chromosome; the smaller chromosome is the Y chromosome. The body cells of a woman carry two X chromosomes; those of a man carry an X chromosome and a Y chromosome.

The figure below shows how a person's sex is inherited.

Note

- a baby's sex depends on whether the egg is fertilised by a sperm carrying an X chromosome or one carrying a Y chromosome
- the birth of (almost) equal numbers of girls and boys is governed by the production of equal numbers of X and Y sperms at meiosis.

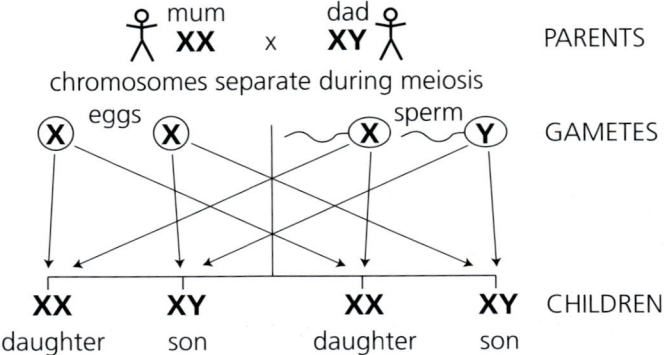

Exam tips

Remember that the sex of a person depends on whether a sperm with an **X chromosome** or **Y chromosome** fertilises the egg. Dad is responsible for the child being a boy or a girl! Also **remember** that meiosis determines the 50:50 ratio of boys to girls.

See also • p. 30 **Meiosis**

Sex-linked inheritance

Characteristics controlled by alleles situated on the sex chromosomes are said to be **sex-linked** characteristics. The disease **haemophilia** is an example. The figure below shows what happens.

The outcome when a man affected by haemophilia becomes a father

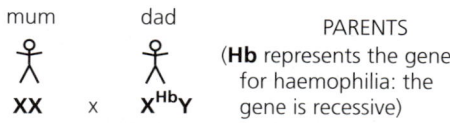

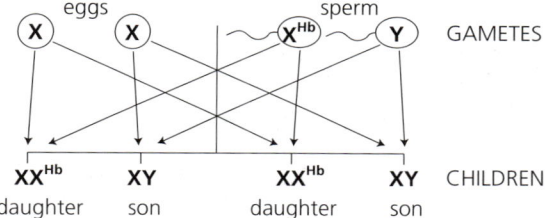

Outcome: the children are not affected by haemophilia but the two daughters are **carriers** of the haemophilia gene.

The outcome when a woman who is a carrier of the haemophilia allele becomes a mother

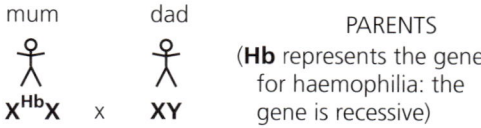

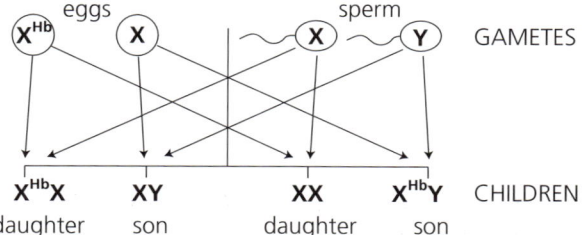

Outcome: one daughter is a **carrier** of the haemophilia gene, one son is affected by haemophilia because the Y chromosome does not carry as many genes as the X chromosome – the recessive haemophilia gene does not have a partner on the Y chromosome to mask its effect.

Genetic engineering

Modern **biotechnology** (the way we use different types of cell to produce useful substances) depends on **genetic engineering**.

- **Restriction enzymes** cut DNA into pieces making it possible to isolate specific genes.
- **Ligase** (splicing enzyme) allows desirable genes to be inserted into the genetic material of host cells.

Using genetic engineering we can create organisms with specific genetic characteristics such that they produce substances that we need and want. The microorganisms are cultured in a solution containing all the substances they require for rapid growth and multiplication inside huge containers called **fermenters**. In this way medicines, foods and industrial chemicals can be made on an industrial scale (see page 91).

- **Batch culture** produces batches of product in a fermenter – the fermenter is then emptied of the product and the nutrient solution and then sterilised with super-heated steam ready for the next batch.
- **Continuous culture** produces substances as an on-going process – the product is drawn off the fermenter and nutrients are replaced as they are used.

Factfile

For thousands of years humans have used the methods of **traditional biotechnology** to make food:
- **yeast** to make wine, beer and bread
- **moulds** to make cheese
- **bacteria** to make yogurt and vinegar.

Exam tips

Remember that the techniques of **biotechnology** use different types of cell to produce substances that are useful to us. **Genetic engineering** is just *one* of many techniques used. It describes the methods of **manipulating genes** to create organisms with useful characteristics.

Making genetically engineered insulin

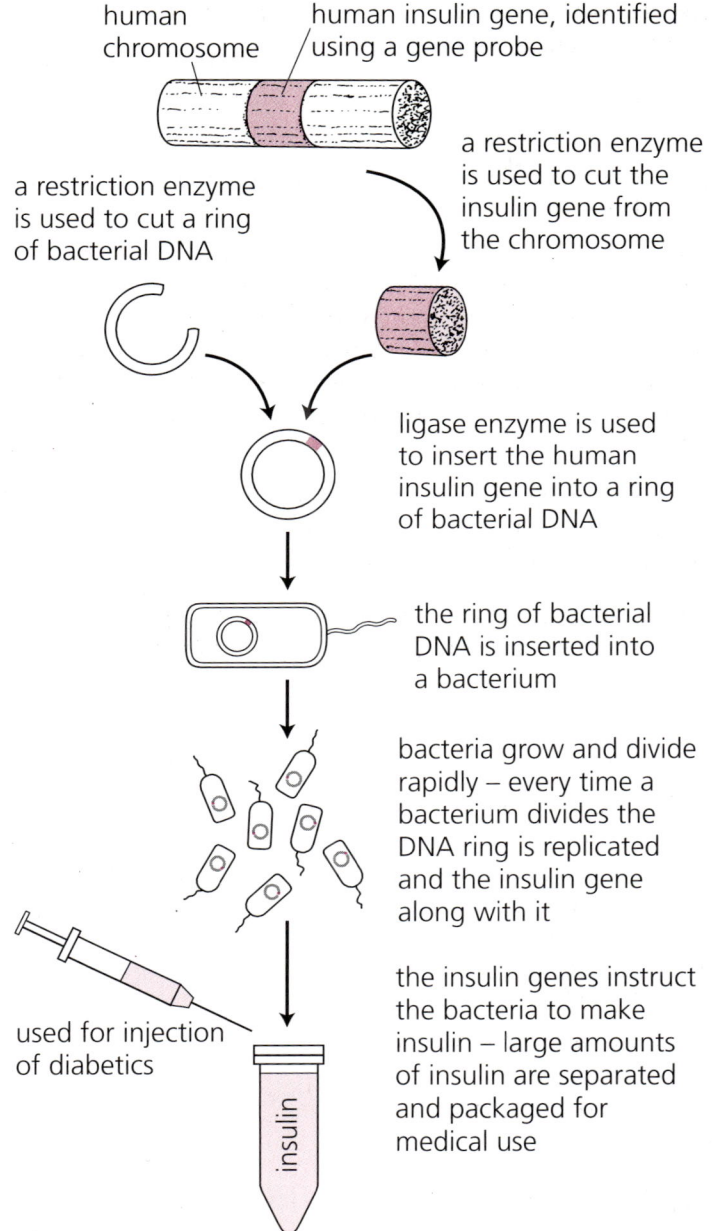

Variation

Differently coloured hair and eyes are examples of the **variations** in the different characteristics which make up an individual's **phenotype**.

Genetic causes of variation:

- **sexual reproduction** – fertilisation recombines the genetic material from each parent in new ways within the **zygote**
- **mutations** arise as a result of mistakes in the **replication** of DNA – **ionising radiation** and some **chemicals** increase the probability of gene mutation
- **crossing over** during **meiosis** exchanges a segment of one chromosome (and the genes it carries) with the corresponding segment of its homologous chromosome.

Variations that arise from genetic causes are inherited and are the raw material on which **natural selection** acts, resulting in **evolution**.

Environmental causes of variation:

- **nutrients** in food affect the size of individuals
- **drugs** may have a serious effect on appearance (e.g. **thalidomide**)
- **temperature** affects the rate of enzyme-controlled chemical reactions, e.g. warmth increases the rate of photosynthesis
- **physical training** uses the muscles more than normal, increasing their size and power.

Variations that arise from environmental causes are not inherited because the sex cells are not affected. Instead the characteristics are said to be **acquired**. Because variations as a result of acquired characteristics are not inherited, they do not affect evolution.

Exam tips

Make sure you can distinguish between **phenotype** and **genotype**:

- phenotype describes the characteristics of a living thing as a result of the expression of genes
- genotype describes the genetic make-up of a living thing; all of its genes, expressed **and** non-expressed.

The variations shown by some characteristics are spread over a range of measurements. All intermediate forms of a characteristic are possible between one extreme and the other. We say that the characteristic shows **continuous variation**.

Variation in the height of the adult human population – an example of continuous variation

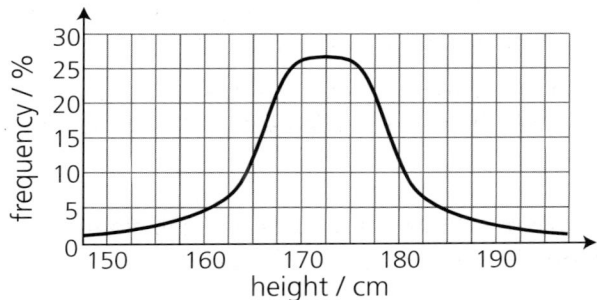

Other characteristics do not show a continuous trend in variation from one extreme to another. They show categories of the characteristic without any intermediate forms. The ability to roll the tongue is an example – you can either do it or you can't. We say that the characteristic shows **discontinuous variation**.

Ability to roll the tongue – an example of discontinuous variation

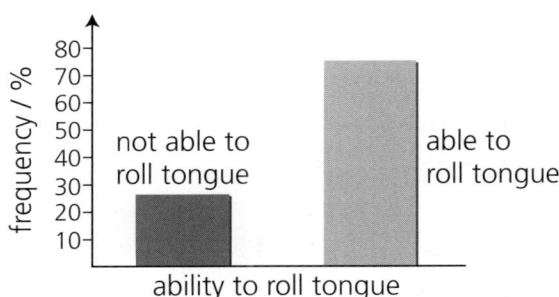

Evolution

Present-day organisms are descended from **ancestors** that have changed through thousands of generations. The process of change is called **evolution**. **Fossils** are the remains of or impressions made by dead organisms. They are **direct** evidence that evolution has taken place.

How species evolve

- because offspring vary genetically, individuals of the same species are slightly different from one another (except identical twins)
- organisms compete for resources in limited supply; variation means that individuals with genes that express characteristics which suit (**adapt**) the individuals to obtain scarce resources are more likely to survive than other less well adapted individuals; the process is called **natural selection** and is the mechanism of evolution
- the best adapted individuals are more likely to survive and reproduce and so their offspring will inherit the genes for those favoured characteristics
- in this way organisms accumulate genes for favourable characteristics and change through time; that is, they **evolve** over many generations
- if the environment in which individuals are living changes – then genes for different characteristics might favour survival; individuals with these characteristics will survive to reproduce and so evolution continues from generation to generation.

The figure on page 95 shows an example of evolution in action.

People behind the science

Charles Darwin (1809–1882) was a keen British naturalist who abandoned medicine at Edinburgh University and studied theology at Cambridge. His world voyage on HMS *Beagle* (1831–36) provided much of the evidence that:

- organisms **evolve** and that
- **natural selection** is the mechanism of evolution.

It was not until 1859 that he published these proposals in his book *The Origin of Species*.

See also • p. 9 **Species** • p. 20 **Competition** • p. 21 **Population**
• p. 86 **Gene expression** • p. 92 **Variation**

Different forms of *Biston betularia* adapt the moth to survive in different environments

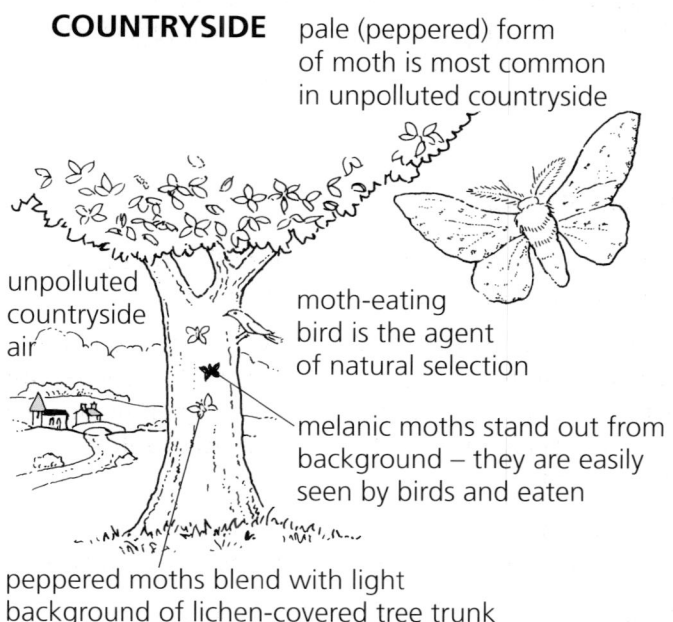

COUNTRYSIDE pale (peppered) form of moth is most common in unpolluted countryside

unpolluted countryside air

moth-eating bird is the agent of natural selection

melanic moths stand out from background – they are easily seen by birds and eaten

peppered moths blend with light background of lichen-covered tree trunk

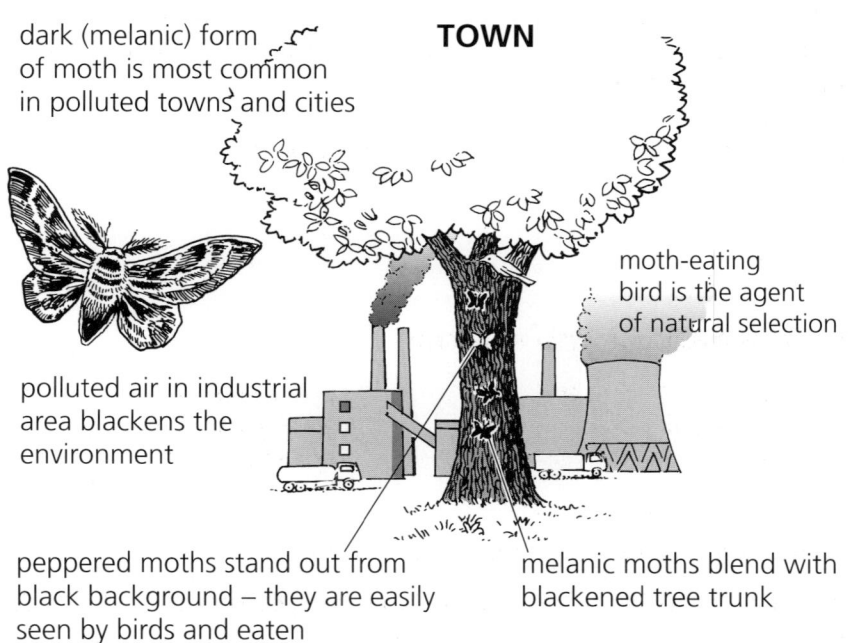

dark (melanic) form of moth is most common in polluted towns and cities

TOWN

moth-eating bird is the agent of natural selection

polluted air in industrial area blackens the environment

peppered moths stand out from black background – they are easily seen by birds and eaten

melanic moths blend with blackened tree trunk

Inheritance and evolution quiz

1. Distinguish between the processes of kneading, proving and baking in the making of bread.
2. What are the advantages to diabetics of using insulin produced by bacteria into which the human insulin gene has been inserted?
3. In humans the gene for brown eyes (**B**) is dominant to the gene for blue eyes (**b**). (a) Using the symbols B and b, state the genotypes of the children that could be born from a heterozygous father and a blue-eyed mother. (b) State whether the children are brown-eyed or blue-eyed.
4. Why are acquired characteristics not inherited?
5. Why does sexual reproduction produce much more genetic variation than asexual reproduction?
6. Distinguish between evolution and natural selection.

Answers

1. kneading – repeated folding of the dough makes spaces which are filled with the carbon dioxide produced by the action of yeast enzymes on the sugar in the dough / proving – carbon dioxide fills the spaces produced by kneading / baking – kills yeast, stopping the action of enzymes / ethanol produced by yeast fermenting sugars is driven off
2. genetically engineered insulin is cheaper; available in large quantities; and chemically the same as human insulin, preventing a possible immune response to injection of the hormone
3. (a) Bb or bb (b) 50% of the children would be brown-eyed; 50% blue-eyed
4. acquired characteristics are those produced in the individual as a result of the influence (effects) of the environment / these characteristics are not the result of genetic influence and are therefore not inherited
5. during sexual reproduction: genetic material inherited from both parents recombines in the fertilised egg producing combinations of genetic material in the offspring different from the combination in each of the parents / during asexual reproduction: offspring inherit identical genetic material from one parent; mutation is the only source of variation
6. evolution – the change that occurs through many generations of descendants from different ancestors / natural selection – the mechanism of evolution through the survival of favourable variations